C000302329

KNOWING ME,
KNOWING GOD

RICHARD
BRASH

'Winsome and rich, this book wonderfully exhibits the bond between the knowledge of God and of ourselves. Richard Brash gives us a reliable compass to keep us from getting lost in the theological forest.'
Michael Horton, J. Gresham Machen Professor of Systematic Theology and Apologetics, Westminster Seminary California, USA

'Thoroughly contemporary but at the same time well rooted in exegesis and biblical theology, this volume quickly gripped me as a fresh, stimulating and enjoyable plea for systematic theology. But it is more than a plea. Its six keys serve as both invaluable entry points and as axioms to guide us in lifelong study of the relations between one biblical truth and another, and between each truth (or Scripture text) and the whole field of revelation. The keys are well chosen and, being presented in pairs, remind us of the danger of being carried away by one side of a truth at the expense of another. This volume will both feed and stretch your mind, but it will not exhaust it.'
Donald Macleod, Edinburgh Theological Seminary

'I don't know of a better introduction to Christian doctrine than this brilliant new book by Richard Brash. It is both modest and ambitious in its aim: not attempting, like a textbook, to cover all the major doctrinal themes, but rather, like a guidebook, seeking to introduce the territory and point us in the right direction to discover its delights. We are introduced to three deceptively simple pairs of contrasting statements, which together provide a window into the vast vista of biblical teaching, a compass that enables us to navigate the terrain, and a set of keys to help us begin to unlock some of the mysteries we meet along the way. This is theology at its best: biblically grounded, mind-blowing and heart-warming. It is a great resource, both for those who are new to systematic theology and to seasoned travellers. Enjoy the journey!'
Vaughan Roberts, Rector of St Ebbe's Church, Oxford, UK, author of *God's Big Picture*

'Many people are wary of "systematic theology" but it is, when done properly, simply an exercise in reading the Bible as a whole and in fellowship with God's people. Richard Brash shows us how that is so. This simple doctrinal "compass" will help you navigate life in God's world in the light of God's Word. Richard writes with a clarity that comes from knowing the subject well. He enables us to see that the big picture of the Bible is both an unfolding narrative and a coherent account of God and his purpose in creating us, making himself known to us, and saving us from sin. Highly recommended.'

Mark D. Thompson, Principal, Moore Theological College, Sydney, Australia

KNOWING ME, KNOWING GOD

SIX THEOLOGICAL KEYS TO SCRIPTURE

RICHARD BRASH

INTER-VARSITY PRESS
36 Causton Street, London SW1P 4ST, England
Email: ivp@ivpbooks.com
Website: www.ivpbooks.com

© Richard Brash, 2021

Richard Brash has asserted his right under the Copyright, Designs and Patents Act, 1988,
to be identified as Author of this work.

All rights reserved. No part of this publication may be reproduced, stored in a retrieval system,
or transmitted, in any form or by any means, electronic, mechanical, photocopying, recording or
otherwise, without the prior permission of the publisher or the Copyright Licensing Agency.

Unless otherwise indicated, Scripture quotations are taken from the ESV Bible (The Holy Bible,
English Standard Version, Anglicized edition), copyright © 2001 by Crossway, a publishing
ministry of Good News Publishers. Used by permission. All rights reserved.

Scripture quotations marked NASB are taken from the NEW AMERICAN STANDARD BIBLE®,
Copyright © 1960, 1962, 1963, 1968, 1971, 1972, 1973, 1975, 1977, 1995 by The Lockman Foundation.
Used by permission.

Scripture quotations marked NET are taken from the NET Bible, New English Translation,
are copyright © 1996 by Biblical Studies Press, LLC. NET Bible is a registered trademark.

Scripture quotations marked NIV are taken from The Holy Bible, New International Version
(Anglicized edition). Copyright © 1979, 1984, 2011 by Biblica. Used by permission of Hodder &
Stoughton Ltd, an Hachette UK company. All rights reserved. 'NIV' is a registered trademark
of Biblica. UK trademark number 1448790.

Extracts from The Book of Common Prayer, the rights in which are vested in the Crown,
are reproduced by permission of the Crown's Patentee, Cambridge University Press.

The publisher and author acknowledge with thanks permission to reproduce extracts
from the following:
Mere Christianity by C. S. Lewis © copyright C. S. Lewis Pte Ltd 1942, 1943, 1944, 1952.
Reflections on the Psalms by C. S. Lewis © copyright C. S. Lewis Pte Ltd 1958.
Every effort has been made to seek permission to use copyright material reproduced in this book.
The publisher apologizes for those cases where permission might not have been sought and,
if notified, will formally seek permission at the earliest opportunity.

First published 2021

British Library Cataloguing-in-Publication Data
A catalogue record for this book is available from the British Library.

ISBN: 978–1–78974–183–4
eBook ISBN: 978–1–78974–184–1

Set in Minion Pro 11/14pt
Typeset in Great Britain by CRB Associates, Potterhanworth, Lincolnshire
Printed and bound in Great Britain by Ashford Colour Press Ltd, Gosport, Hampshire

Produced on paper from sustainable forests.

*Inter-Varsity Press publishes Christian books that are true to the Bible and that communicate
the gospel, develop discipleship and strengthen the church for its mission in the world.*

*IVP originated within the Inter-Varsity Fellowship, now the Universities and Colleges Christian
Fellowship, a student movement connecting Christian Unions in universities and colleges throughout
Great Britain, and a member movement of the International Fellowship of Evangelical Students.
Website: www.uccf.org.uk. That historic association is maintained, and all senior IVP staff and
committee members subscribe to the UCCF Basis of Faith.*

For Yuko
Proverbs 18:22

Contents

Contents

Preface

Nearly all the wisdom which we possess, that is to say, true and sound wisdom, consists of two parts: *the knowledge of God and of ourselves.*[1]

In God you come up against something which is in every respect immeasurably superior to yourself. Unless you know God as that – and, therefore, know yourself as nothing in comparison – you do not know God at all.[2]

This book is about the pursuit of 'true and sound wisdom'. It's written under the conviction that all true wisdom comes from God and may be found, supremely, in the Bible. John Calvin was right: if we would be truly wise, we need to know God *and* we need to know ourselves. God is the source of the whole, and the two parts cannot finally be separated. Rather, each illuminates the other. Calvin's famous maxim will serve as a guide as we go along.[3]

Biblically speaking, 'wisdom' is not the preserve of an intellectual elite. Nor is it meant to be shut up in books. It is a way of life, even *the* Way of life (1 Cor. 1:24). It begins with the fear of God (Prov. 9:10). And it's accompanied by joy (Eccl. 2:26) – the gift of joy in the Lord that is the delightful privilege of God's children through Jesus Christ.

---

1 John Calvin, *Institutes of the Christian Religion*, edited by John T. McNeill (Louisville: Westminster John Knox, 1960), I.1.i; emphasis added.

2 C. S. Lewis, *Mere Christianity* (New York: Touchstone: 1996; first published 1952), 111; cited in Kelly M. Kapic, *A Little Book for New Theologians: How and Why to Study Theology* (Downers Grove: InterVarsity Press, 2012), 73.

3 This book therefore represents an exercise in what Kelly Kapic calls 'anthroposensitive' theology, with a double focus on (i) God and (ii) our lives in relation to God. See Kapic, *Little Book*, 47–48.

Knowing me and *knowing God* are corporate endeavours, not solitary pursuits. As I'll explain later in this book, knowing 'me' includes knowing (and ultimately loving) my fellow human beings. We receive wisdom as we participate in the 'communion of saints', both living and dead.

Among the dead, I'm grateful to the seventeenth-century Puritan John Owen. I've learned more from Owen about the grace and glory of the God who has given himself to us in the gifts of his Son and his Spirit, than I have from anyone else. Owen's works have been my steady companion as I've written this book. Another brilliant theological John – John Webster – offered encouragement to me by email in the early days of my graduate studies, and then following his untimely death in 2016 became the subject of my PhD thesis. Even when I have at times disagreed with him, I've been grateful for Webster's steady guidance in the work of theology, a work he described as that 'delightful activity in which the Church praises God by ordering its thinking towards the gospel of Christ'.[4]

Among the living, I'm particularly grateful to my seminary teachers in Tokyo (Japan Bible Seminary) and London (Westminster Theological Seminary and London Theological Seminary), and to my brother (and 'father') pastor-teachers in Oxford and Edinburgh, who have modelled careful attention to Scripture in their ministries, and a commitment to living all of life for the glory of God.

My wife, Yuko, has been my closest friend for the last twenty years. Ever the 'practical' theologian, she has also usually been the first to ask me the all-important question 'So what?' To judge by recent experience, our children Kaz and Isla are following in her footsteps!

I wish also to acknowledge the contributions of others in the actual writing and production of this book. Much of it was written in the Hewat Room at New College in the University of Edinburgh, punctuated by conversations with other PhD students, especially B. J. Condrey and Karl Dahlfred. Andrew Curry and Vaughan Roberts kindly read and commented on an early draft of the

---

4   John Webster, *Holiness* (Grand Rapids: Eerdmans, 2003), 8.

manuscript and suggested various corrections and additions, some of which I have gratefully incorporated here. I'm grateful to Phil Duce, Senior Commissioning Editor at Inter-Varsity Press, for his big-picture advice and careful eye for details. However, all responsibility for the finished work is mine.

Whether *knowing me* or *knowing God*, it's my experience that good books can be a help along the way. This book has been written to help you in your pursuit of 'true and sound wisdom', in the company of the saints. May you, the reader, grow in grace and knowledge, to the glory of God.

Note: This book is not an academic book, but it does make use of some technical terms. I try to define briefly or explain such terms when they first appear. There is also a glossary at the back of the book, which readers may find useful for reference. In addition, there are more than 200 footnotes. Most of these acknowledge references to other books. Some suggest further reading. Others offer help with definitions. The occasional lengthier footnote may follow up an interesting side point or give more detailed evidence, sometimes at a more complex level. These longer footnotes are not essential to the argument of the book: please feel free to ignore them if you prefer.

Each chapter concludes with some questions for personal reflection and application. These questions would equally be suitable for a discussion based on the chapter.

Bible citations are from the English Standard Version (ESV) unless otherwise stated.

Abbreviations

AD	Anno Domini (in the year of the Lord)
BDAG	Bauer, W., F. W. Danker, W. F. Arndt and F. W. Gingrich, *A Greek-English Lexicon of the New Testament and Other Early Christian Literature*, 3rd edn (Chicago: University of Chicago Press, 2000)
c.	circa
ESV	English Standard Version
HALOT	L. Koehler and W. Baumgartner, *The Hebrew and Aramaic Lexicon of the Old Testament*, 5 vols. (Leiden: Brill, 1994–2000)
NASB	New American Standard Bible
NET	New English Translation
NIV	New International Version
NRSV	New Revised Standard Version
Q	Question
s.v.	sub voce (under the word or heading)

Introduction

What is 'systematic theology'?

Where is Jesus? It took a child – my own son, in fact – to ask the question that nearly floored me. 'You said just now that he's in heaven, but the Sunday club teacher told us he's everywhere.' Before I even had a chance to think, he landed another unexpected punch: 'And in our family worship time the other day, you said Jesus lives in our hearts!'

Well . . . where *is* Jesus? Preachers may tell us we can find Jesus in the Bible. One well-known evangelist likes to say that Jesus 'walks off the pages' of Scripture. Is Jesus there too? If all four are true – he's in heaven, he's everywhere, he's in our hearts, and he's in the Bible – what possible explanation can we give that makes sense of it all?

Recently, I was sitting in on a youth Bible study. It was all about how God is triune: three and one. The teacher – who also seemed to be decidedly youthful – explained, 'God is like a man who is a husband, and a dad and a friend, all at the same time. He's always a husband and always a dad and always a friend, but he's only ever one man. He's three-in-one.'

Is that right? *Is* that what God is like? What do you think? How would you explain it?

When I was a student pastor, a young man came to talk to me one day in some obvious distress. He believed in Jesus, and he understood the gospel, but he was concerned that his life didn't seem to measure up to his profession, so he didn't have assurance of salvation. He asked me, 'Do I have to love other people to be a Christian? Because I don't think I do.'

This young man was deadly serious. For him, the question was no idle speculation. It was extremely important. What was I to say to him?

All of these examples concern questions of what is called 'systematic theology'.[1] I study, write and teach systematic theology. As a pastor, I've drawn on the resources of systematic theology to inform my ministry. As a Christian believer who follows Jesus, I seek to allow systematic theology to shape my life. I think it's important – clearly. But I can't assume that you do. Because the reality I've seen is that *many Christians* (perhaps especially *evangelical* Christians) *dislike systematic theology*. When I tell Christian friends that I study, or teach, systematic theology, they are sometimes a bit suspicious.

Why should that be? There are three main reasons or objections that I've heard. First, some Christians wonder whether *any* sort of theology is really necessary. Isn't theology just a distraction – they might ask – from the Bible (on the one hand) and from following Jesus (on the other hand)? Second, others might be convinced that *good* theology is better than *no* theology, but they'll say they prefer 'biblical' theology to 'systematic' theology. (I'll explain these terms and the thinking that's going on here in a moment.) Third, still others are worried that theological 'systems' can get too big for their boots, becoming more authoritative than Scripture itself. The fear is that the theological tail might start wagging the biblical dog. These are all important objections, and so I'm going to try to deal with them first, in order to clear the way for what follows in the rest of this book.

Do we really need theology at all?

I remember one woman's prayer for Christians in Japan at a missions conference: 'Lord, please deliver the Japanese from a faith that is dry, and dusty, and theological. Amen.'

In that believer's view – and perhaps in her experience too – 'theology' was almost a synonym for 'dry and dusty'. Or at least all

---

1 Systematic theology (or 'systematics') is sometimes called 'dogmatic theology' (or 'dogmatics'). Some people draw a distinction between these terms. For the purposes of this book I'll treat them as different names for the same thing. Some would say that the last of my three examples above is, more properly, the concern of 'pastoral' theology. In its application to this particular individual that may well be so, but the underlying question ('What is a true Christian?') is one for systematic theology.

three of these things – dryness, dustiness and being 'theological' – were plagues to be avoided at all costs, even to be prayed against.

It is true: theology *can* be dry and dusty, and theologians don't always help in this regard. As a seminary student in Japan, I was put in charge of the library for a semester. During the summer months we would commonly experience 100% humidity,[2] so we had to operate several dehumidifiers to remove the moisture from the air and protect the books. In other words, my job was to *keep* the theological books dry!

I'll admit that the *content* of theology books can be dry too: uninspiring, unedifying and unhelpful. Unfortunately, I've read plenty of books like that. I hope I can be delivered from writing any of them. If theology isn't characterized by truth and love, it can be not only dry and dusty, but also dangerous and divisive.

But the existence of *bad* theology isn't a good reason to reject theology altogether.

There's a meme that's been doing the rounds on my social media feeds recently. Two men are talking. One says, 'I don't need theology. I just need Jesus.' The other man replies, 'I see. So who is this Jesus?' The first man starts to explain, 'He's God incarnate, who came to save mankind from sin and . . .' At which point his friend interrupts him: 'You're doing theology!'

When I lived in London, I remember a friend at church telling me, 'We don't need theology. We just need the Bible.' I have some sympathy for this. As Protestants, we take our stand on the principle *sola Scriptura* (Scripture alone). The Bible is our highest authority for all matters of life and doctrine. But whatever 'Scripture alone' means, it cannot mean that we receive Scripture as it were in a vacuum, with nothing else alongside it. Scripture itself is full of theological statements, and these need to be received, interpreted and digested by human beings, whose minds are themselves informed by principles of logic and other disciplines. We can't really get far in the Christian life if all we do is quote the Bible at each other.

---

2 Coming from 'temperate' Scotland, this was an entirely new concept to me, not least because I assumed that 100% humidity means you must be under water!

Just imagine the conversation after church at the coffee table:

CHRIS: 'Give me a drink' (John 4:7).

CHRISTINE: 'What shall we drink?' (Exod. 15:24). 'Be careful and drink no wine or strong drink' (Judg. 13:4).

CHRIS: 'Please give me a little water to drink from your jar' (Gen. 24:17).

CHRISTINE: 'All drink that could be drunk from every such vessel shall be unclean' (Lev. 11:34).

CHRIS: 'Fool!' (Luke 12:20). 'Give drink to the congregation' (Num. 20:8).

CHRISTINE: 'Let the one who is thirsty come!' (Rev. 22:17).

I know this is a silly example. The last thing I want to do is belittle the words of the Bible. I should be speaking them (and living and breathing them) more than I do. The written Word of God is our daily bread, nourishing us so that we are equipped for every good work.[3] It's great to share (meaningful) Bible verses with our friends or on social media. We should read and memorize as much Scripture as we can.

But it is reductionist to suggest that we can get by – and truly love God with 'all our mind' (see Matt. 22:37) – with Scripture and *nothing* else. In point of fact, this has often been the claim of heretics, who have rejected 'doctrine' in favour of 'nothing but the Bible' or the supposedly 'plain' teaching of (usually particular verses of) Scripture.[4]

The truth is: *we all do theology*. We all 'have' a theology. Some theologies are, I take it, better than others. The Lord Jesus had, and has, a theology. *God* has a theology. (Does that sound strange? More

---

3　Deut. 8:3; Matt. 4:4; 2 Tim. 3:17. In the Bible, God has preserved for us all the words we need for true life: there is nothing comparable to Scripture! On God's preservation of Scripture for us see particularly ch. 4 of my book *A Christian's Pocket Guide to How God Preserved the Bible* (Fearn: Christian Focus, 2019).

4　Examples would be the fourth-century Arians, who denied the divinity of Jesus, and the sixteenth- and seventeenth-century Socinians, who denied key orthodox doctrines such as the pre-existence of Christ, the Trinity, a historical fall, original sin, penal substitutionary atonement and God's omniscience (knowledge of all things). Both groups claimed to be following the 'plain' teaching of Scripture.

on this later.) There's a sense in which even non-Christians have a theology, as I hope to show you. The question should be, therefore, not 'Do I need theology?' but 'Is my theology any good?'

Isn't 'biblical' theology enough?

Sometimes, people in churches have said to me something like 'I prefer **biblical** theology to **systematic** theology.'

When I ask what they mean by that, it often seems that they think biblical theology is, by definition, more 'biblical' than systematic theology.

Names can be misleading. Evangelicals aim – rightly – to be 'biblical' people. We want to base our life and doctrine on the written Word of God. So, if we're going to do theology, surely we want to do 'biblical' theology. Right?

That's right! But – properly understood – biblical theology and systematic theology can both be equally 'biblical': derived from, and under the authority of, Scripture. It's just that the interpretative lens for approaching the Bible is different.

For biblical theology, that lens is *chrono-logical*. The focus is on the *story* of God's relationship with his people over *time*. For systematic theology, the lens is *theo-logical*.[5] This means that systematics is primarily concerned with the identities of, and relationships between, God and his creatures in the basic categories of *being, knowing and acting*.

Faithful biblical theologians and systematic theologians read, and seek to understand, systematize and teach, the same Bible.[6] But they do so by applying different lenses: whether *chrono-logic*

---

5 *Chronos* is the Greek word for 'time'. *Theos* is the Greek word for 'God'. Of course, there's a sense in which biblical theology is also 'theological'. But I use the terms 'theo-logic' and 'theological' in this book to describe the particular approach to Scripture of systematic theology, with its characteristic concerns in the areas of metaphysics (the nature of reality) and the relationships between God and human beings.

6 I recognize that there are all kinds of 'systematic' theology out there, including 'feminist', 'liberation', 'black' and 'queer' varieties. I don't think that there's *nothing* to learn from these approaches, but on the other hand I'd argue it's safe to say we can learn *almost nothing* of Calvin's 'true and sound wisdom' from these approaches to systematic theology. That is because they do not take the Bible as their starting point or final authority.

(biblical theology), or what we might call *theo-logic* (systematic theology).

So, the name 'biblical theology' is actually a bit unfortunate. One well-known evangelical theological college currently offers a 'Diploma in Biblical Theology'. But a closer look at the module units on offer reveals that some of them are, more properly, courses in systematic theology or historical theology. The desire to be 'biblical' in our theology is a good one. But systematic theology can – and should – be just as 'biblical' as biblical theology.

I want to suggest that when we read the Bible, we need to learn from *both* a *chrono*-logical *and* a *theo*-logical approach. Why? Because these are the two perspectives on any story (including the Bible's story) that give us true understanding of it. If we neglect one or other of them, we can end up with serious misunderstandings. Conversely, when we allow these two complementary perspectives to inform and enrich each other, fruitful growth may follow.

Every weekday morning, my wife and I watch a 15-minute episode of the 'morning drama' produced by NHK, Japan's public broadcaster. The 'morning drama' story changes every six months, but the programmes have been running since 1961, and still command an audience share of up to 20% in Japan. Every quarter, NHK publishes a magazine to complement the current series. Half of the magazine tells the (chronological) story, so that you can keep up to date, or remind yourself what's happened. The other half is filled with 'character profiles' and diagrams that map out the (sometimes complicated) relationships between the characters.

Here's the point: if you want to understand the drama properly, *both* halves of the magazine are important. For example, it's useful to know that in episode 102, the main character moves in next door to an old man she doesn't recognize. But it's also helpful to know that the old man is blind. And short-tempered. And that he happens to be the grandfather of the main character's best friend, who once double-crossed her own mother's school teacher back in episode 46 (or whatever).

If we're to make sense of the story, we need to know *both* the events that happen in some sort of chronological order *and* the identities of, and relationships between, the characters in the story. This includes what the characters tell us, or reveal, about themselves, although sometimes we as viewers or readers are made privy to information about the characters by the narrator, which even the characters themselves are not aware of.

When it comes to the story of the Bible, then, we need the help of both biblical *and* systematic theology.[7] It goes without saying that the story of the Bible is more important than any drama on television. In addition, the Bible's story is different from most other stories in that *we are invited to become characters in the continuing story that the Bible tells.* Part of understanding the Bible is therefore understanding not just who *God* is, but who *we* are as human beings, and what our relationship with God is, or can be.

I'm not suggesting here that systematic theology is *only* about characters and relationships. Doctrines encompass other things as well, including metaphysical truth claims, historical events and knowledge of 'things' in the world. However, the focus on characters and relationships in this book should be a healthy corrective to the view that doctrine is somehow 'propositional' but not 'personal'. As will become clear in this book, I don't think this is a sustainable antithesis. Good systematic theology keeps these two things closely together.[8]

7　There are other helpful ways of describing the relationship between biblical and systematic theology. The great nineteenth-century Scottish preacher Thomas Guthrie compared biblical theology to a natural landscape in which the various plants and flowers are found 'in ordered disorder'. In contrast, he compared systematic theology to a botanical garden where plants and flowers are gathered and arranged according to species. As T. C. Hammond comments on this distinction, 'The former is pleasing to the eye. The latter is suited for that closer study which opens to us the secrets of nature.' See T. C. Hammond, *In Understanding Be Men: A Handbook of Christian Doctrine*, edited and revised by David F. Wright (London: Inter-Varsity Press, 1968), 13.

　　More recently, A. N. Williams has argued helpfully that a truly *systematic* theology will deal with not just doctrine by doctrine in turn, but the *logical interrelationships* between doctrines. See *The Architecture of Theology: Structure, System, and Ratio* (Oxford: Oxford University Press, 2011), 1–4.

8　'Complete' systematic theologies (if such endeavours are possible) will include treatment of other biblical characters who are neither God nor human beings, namely angels and demons. There is a place also for animals and other creatures in systematic theology. However, for the most part I will pass over such subjects in this book. That said, a biblically informed understanding of *who God is* and *who we are* (and *how we relate to God*) ought to inform what Christians think and do about such issues as the global climate crisis and other environmental concerns that cannot be covered here.

What all this means is that the common evangelical dislike (or perhaps 'mistrust') of systematic theology isn't necessarily justified. We *all* have a systematic theology, because we all try to think logical thoughts about God, and relate to him in ways that make sense to us. Our aim in doing systematic theology (just as in biblical theology) should be to let God teach us through the Bible, so that we can understand, know, love, worship, live for, share and teach *the God of the Bible* in the Spirit and in truth.[9] For that is the life of blessing: even eternal life!

What happens if the system takes over?

One more common concern about systematic theology is that our systems might become more authoritative than Scripture itself. If parts of the Bible don't seem to 'fit' whatever our systematic theology teaches, those sections of Scripture are (it is claimed) reinterpreted so as to fit them into the system. The danger is that we end up preserving and defending the system at all costs.

This concern is real. If we approach Scripture with a certain set of authoritative ideas as to what it's all about, there's a risk we'll simply find what we're looking for, and much of what *is* there will pass us over.

On the other hand, as evangelicals we should believe that the Bible itself can and must be systematized. Why? Because all Scripture is the inspired Word of God, and so it reflects God's self-understanding. God's own knowledge is, by definition, true and fully coherent: it is therefore *systematic*. And, as we'll see in chapters 3 and 4, it's a measure of precisely this divine knowledge that God wants to communicate to us. This is our starting point, then: the Bible *can't* be full of logical contradictions, teaching one thing one day and the opposite the next. With God's illuminating help, the Bible is *able* to be systematized by its readers: indeed, it *demands* to be systematized!

As I've already suggested, we all have a systematic theology of our own, whether we recognize it as such or not. In other words, there

---

9   With the NIV, I take *pneuma* (spirit) in the second part of John 4:24 to be a reference to the Holy Spirit.

are things we think we know about God and about ourselves, and when we read the Bible we inevitably read in the light of prior knowledge. This means that *Christian* Bible-reading should be an experience, over time, of having 'our' theology better and better conformed to God's theology. This is the work of the Holy Spirit, and it's not usually something we do all by ourselves but in partnership/fellowship with other believers, including our forebears in the faith.

How does this partnership work? Over the years, Christians have drawn up various 'subordinate' standards as keys or guidelines to help them interpret Scripture correctly. At their best, these keys have always arisen out of Scripture's own teaching. For example, the early church had something they called the 'analogy of faith'.[10] Based on Romans 12:6 (which says, in the ESV, that an individual Christian must exercise the gift of prophecy 'in proportion to his faith': more literally, this is 'according to the analogy of faith'), the 'analogy of faith' seems to have been a statement of faith along the lines of the Apostles' Creed. It acted as a kind of litmus test for faithful Bible interpretation and teaching. Later, church councils drew up a range of creeds, such as the Nicene and Athanasian creeds, to guard against various heresies. At the time of the Reformation and in the following decades, churches produced more detailed 'confessions of faith' (like the *Westminster Confession of Faith*, 1646). A more recent example of an evangelical 'subordinate standard' would be the *Chicago Statement on Biblical Inerrancy* (1978).[11]

As evangelicals, we should not be afraid of such subordinate standards. They need not compromise *sola Scriptura*. In fact, they can help us to defend and define it,[12] just as they can help us to formulate systematic theology in ways that will foster gospel growth

---

10 In Latin, this is called the *regula fidei* (rule of faith). It is found as early as the works of Irenaeus of Lyons (c. 130–202). As Keith Mathison demonstrates, for thinkers like Augustine (354–430) the rule of faith was 'essentially a summary of Holy Scripture'. See Keith A. Mathison, *The Shape of Sola Scriptura* (Moscow, Idaho: Canon, 2001), 40.

11 The text of the statement is available online, <https://library.dts.edu/Pages/TL/Special/ICBI_1.pdf>. Accessed 14 June 2019.

12 Mathison's book cited above is a brilliant defence of *sola Scriptura*, as opposed to both Roman Catholicism's view *and* the view that we need *nothing* but the Bible. I commend it highly.

in our lives, following our forebears. As we develop in systematic understanding of Scripture, with the help of subordinate standards, our systems should be in constant dialogue with the Bible itself. We should be aware of both how the system arises *from* Scripture, and how the system in turn helps us go back *to* Scripture with greater understanding of the whole. This will ensure that our system is both quickened and chastened by God's written Word.

Where does this book fit in?

We are blessed today with a number of relatively simple, but still excellent, books that aim to summarize the story of the Bible *chronologically*. One of my favourites is Vaughan Roberts's book *God's Big Picture*.[13] I first read Vaughan's book when it was published in 2003. I used it as a basis for teaching a group at our church in Glasgow in 2005. Later, in God's providence, Vaughan was my boss when I worked at St Ebbe's Church in Oxford from 2012 to 2017. I even 'stood in' for Vaughan a couple of times while he was teaching *God's Big Picture* in the local ministry training course, so I became very familiar with the book.

God's Big Picture is an excellent resource for understanding the story of the Bible. It's a great example of biblical theology done faithfully and concisely, for the benefit of the church. Perhaps its greatest strength is that it really is an *overview*. You won't find detailed discussion of Lamentations or 3 John in *God's Big Picture*. But you will get a clear grasp of the outline of the Bible's story, or a framework to work with, so that as you get deeper into the Bible you know where the different parts fit in and how they fit together.

Another helpful '*chrono*-logic key' for understanding the Bible's story is the four-part progression *Creation – Fall – Redemption – Restoration*.[14] This has recently been popularized by writers and

---

13 Vaughan Roberts, *God's Big Picture: Tracing the Storyline of the Bible* (Leicester: Inter-Varsity Press, 2003).

14 In some versions, 'restoration' is 'consummation'. The underlying chrono-logic is unchanged by the different terminology.

speakers such as John Stott and Tim Keller, and can be found as the basic structure for many a contemporary book and sermon.[15]

Here's my problem: I've struggled to find an equivalent to *God's Big Picture* or the four-part story for systematic theology. Systematic theology textbooks – even the 'introductory' ones – tend to be big and bulky. There's been a distinct lack of a suitable primer to share with friends or students. That's where this book comes in.

In this book, as I've hinted above, I'll be presenting you with a *theological framework for interpreting Scripture, which* (I hope to show you) *arises from Scripture itself,* rather than being imposed on the Bible from outside.

Remember going tenpin bowling when you were a child? It was frustrating when your bowling ball landed in one of the gutters either side of the lane. But if you were lucky, someone helped you by putting guard rails in the gutters to stop your ball going off course. If your bowling ball was headed for the gutter, it would bounce back into the middle of the lane. You might not score a strike every time, but you were pretty much guaranteed to hit *something*! Think of this book as a set of theological guard rails for Bible reading. The rails will help you keep on track. The rails are not to be confused with the bowling pins themselves. You're not aiming to 'hit' or 'arrive at' the six keys around which this book is based. Rather, these keys will help keep you on track, as the Holy Spirit teaches you through (ideally) Jesus' appointed teachers, in the context of a believing church.

So, this isn't a textbook of systematic theology, just as *God's Big Picture* isn't a textbook of biblical theology. Instead, it's intended as both an entry point, and as a conceptual/doctrinal *compass* to guide you through the Bible, in the pursuit of true wisdom. David and

---

15 For a detailed exposition see Trevin Wax, *Counterfeit Gospels: Rediscovering the Good News in a World of False Hope* (Chicago: Moody, 2011), 30–39. There is an account of a 'fourfold framework' to Scripture's story in the introduction to John Stott, *Issues Facing Christians Today* (Grand Rapids: Zondervan, 1984). I'm grateful to Vaughan Roberts for directing me to this. Something similar is also the organizing principle of accounts of the Bible's 'story' as early as Irenaeus (c. 130–202), and is discernible in the most significant theologies of the Western tradition such as those of Augustine, Aquinas and Calvin.

Jonathan Gibson have observed, in cartographic terms, that '[s]ome of the most enduring theological thinking that the church has produced over the centuries has understood itself to be a doctrinal map produced from the biblical terrain in order to be a guide to the biblical terrain'.[16] The Gibson brothers suggest Calvin's *Institutes of the Christian Religion* – surely one of the most significant books of theology ever written – as their prime example of such a doctrinal map. I should make it clear that my book makes no claims to rival Calvin. Unlike Calvin, who is complete and comprehensive, I'm concerned with being brief and basic. This book doesn't attempt to discuss, or even introduce, every Christian doctrine. That's why, although I like the 'map' idea, I prefer to think of this particular book as more like a compass. The compass 'orients' you so that you can relate the map to the (biblical) terrain, and discern how to proceed.

To change the metaphor, I want to give you the systematic-theology 'tools' or 'keys' that you can bring to the various interpretative and theological questions about God and human beings (including of course yourself) that arise as you read the Bible. And I want to do this in as simple and memorable a form as possible.

Every book needs a structure, and every overview needs a key concept or motif that helps hold it all together. For *God's Big Picture*, Vaughan Roberts chose the motif of 'the Kingdom of God'.[17] As a structure for this book, I've chosen three pairs of apparently (but in

---

16 David Gibson and Jonathan Gibson (eds.), *From Heaven He Came and Sought Her: Definite Atonement in Historical, Biblical, Theological, and Pastoral Perspective* (Wheaton: Crossway, 2013), 39. As the Gibson brothers explain, the best kind of map (and, I would add, compass) 'is not a conceptually alien guide to the Bible, nor is it meant to be a hermeneutical grid forced on top of the Bible. Where it functions well, a doctrinal map grows organically out of the biblical parts and enables a bird's-eye view of the canonical whole' (ibid. 40). They also make the important point that a doctrinal map is '[t]o be used as a tool, it is servant not master' (ibid. 40, n.).

17 Another excellent, simple, overview of biblical theology that uses a different motif to that of *God's Big Picture* (in this case, 'covenant') is Jonty Rhodes, *Raiding the Lost Ark: Recovering the Gospel of the Covenant King* (Nottingham: Inter-Varsity Press, 2013). In the USA, this book was published as *Covenants Made Simple: Understanding God's Unfolding Promises to His People* (Phillipsburg: P&R, 2014). The motif of 'covenant' is, in my opinion, singularly effective in bringing together some of the concerns of biblical and systematic theology.

fact not) contradictory theological principles. I've called them six theological 'keys' to Scripture.

The Bible contains many ideas that are, on the surface, contradictory. Some of these instances are clearly deliberate on the part of particular biblical authors. For example, on an apparently mundane level, consider these consecutive verses in the Old Testament book of Proverbs:

> Answer not a fool according to his folly,
>   lest you be like him yourself.
> Answer a fool according to his folly,
>   lest he be wise in his own eyes.
> (Prov. 26:4–5)

Well, which is it? Should we answer a fool according to his folly or not? The answer is, *it depends*. We find wisdom when we consider both sides of the story.

What about this (arguably more important) example, comparing verses in John's Gospel:

> No one has ever seen God . . .
> (John 1:18)

> Jesus said to [Philip], '. . . Whoever has seen me has seen the Father.'
> (John 14:9)

At face value, there's another apparent contradiction here. Has anyone ever seen God, or not? Which is it? In fact, the answer is, once more, *it depends*. Discovering the truth requires that we consider both statements. My principle in this book will be to follow the great English preacher Charles Simeon (1759–1836), who said, 'the truth is *not in the middle*, and *not in one extreme*; but in *both extremes*'.[18]

---

18 Charles Simeon, *Memoirs* (London: J. Hatchard & Son, 1847), 600; emphasis original.

There are many possible examples of this so-called dialectic in the Bible that we might think about.[19] For example, at the level of theological concepts we have the hard-to-reconcile ideas of God's sovereignty and human responsibility, or the statement that God desires 'all people' to be saved alongside the reality that not all will be saved, or John's insistence that the Christian does not keep on sinning (1 John 2:1) juxtaposed with Paul's acknowledgement of his ongoing battle with indwelling sin (Rom. 7:20–24). At the level of our everyday Christian lives we're told that all our sins are forgiven for ever when we believe in Jesus, but we're encouraged to keep on confessing our sins. Or we're told that if we ask God, he will give us what we ask for, but this is not always our experience.[20]

The six theological keys

For this book, I've chosen just three 'foundational' dialectic pairs of principles in the Bible. Each pair will have two chapters: one for each principle. Together, these make up our six theological keys to Scripture. Here they are:

1 God is not like us.
2 God has made us like himself.
3 We cannot comprehend God.
4 God makes himself known to us.
5 Our sin separates us from God.
6 God overcomes sin and makes us his own.

---

19 *Dialectic* means a way of discovering what is true by considering opposites. Perhaps I need to be clear – for the benefit of some readers – that I use the word 'dialectic' differently from the way it's been used in some philosophy or theology. The German idealist philosopher Hegel was famous for his 'dialectic', according to which every thesis has an antithesis, and together these lead us to a synthesis. Hegel has been accused of pantheism (the doctrine that everything is God) and even though he denied this charge, he certainly did not teach orthodox (true) Christianity. Twentieth-century theologian Karl Barth was known for his 'dialectical theology', which at times ended up far away from the Bible's teaching. The dialectics I'll be talking about in this book are strictly biblical. In each case, both sides of the dialectic are taught in Scripture, and we do not move 'beyond' them to some other understanding. Both aspects must be maintained.

20 These examples, and several others, are included in Robert S. Rayburn's helpful 2017 article 'The Dialectical Nature of Biblical Revelation', <https://www.faithtacoma.org/changedmind/the-dialectical-nature-of-biblical-revelation>. Accessed 10 May 2019.

There's a deep-level reason for my choice of these three dialectics. Each 'pair' of statements relates to one of the three foundational categories within which we can understand the identities of, and relationships between, God and his people: **being, knowing** and **acting**.

The first pair (God is not like us / God has made us like himself) is about *being*, or, in technical terms, 'ontology'. By exploring these statements systematically, we can find out what the Bible teaches about God's identity, our own identity as human beings and how these identities relate. According to the Bible, our identity is given to us: we don't need to make it up. That's good news!

The second pair (We cannot comprehend God / God makes himself known to us) is about *knowing*, or, in technical terms, 'epistemology'. As we get into what the Bible teaches in line with these statements, we'll be able to understand what it means to know (for God and for us) and how it is possible for finite human creatures to have knowledge of an infinite God.

The third pair (Our sin separates us from God / God overcomes sin and makes us his own) is about *acting*,[21] or in technical terms 'ethics' and 'soteriology' (salvation). In these final two chapters, we will consider the teaching of Scripture about what we *ought* to do and what we *actually* do – in the past, present and future – and what *God* has done, is doing, and will do in respect of us.

As should be clear from the reference to past, present and future in the last paragraph, it is ultimately impossible (and in fact undesirable) to separate systematic theology entirely from *chronological* considerations. For a start, we are time-bound creatures, and we cannot observe either God or ourselves from 'outside' time. The story on the one hand, and the characters and their relationships on the other (or *chrono-logic* and *theo-logic*) complement each other, and come together to illuminate each other as well. Nor can we completely separate being, knowing and acting. We are human *beings*,

---

21 By 'acting' I mean simply 'doing', rather than 'putting on a performance'. I prefer the word 'acting' to 'doing' because it clearly indicates *willing intention* to do something. Both God and human 'agents' can act, in accordance with their respective wills. More on this in chapter 5.

after all, and it is a necessary consequence of our *being* that we should *know* and *act*. If this book serves to help you – as a Bible reader – to integrate some of these things in your own understanding when you read Scripture so that you know God and yourself better, then it will have served its main purpose.

Beyond that, I dare to hope that you might be encouraged to live differently in the light of what you read. As American theologian Michael Horton reminds us, the Bible's *drama* (essentially, the *story* that is at the heart of biblical theology, into which we are invited) and its *doctrine* (which is the main subject of systematic theology) always go hand in hand with *doxology* (giving glory to God) and *discipleship* (following Jesus Christ in willing obedience).[22] Doctrine studied for its own sake is of little value: indeed, such study may even serve to calcify or harden our hearts. As we go through, I hope to show you that the keys in this book offer just the safeguards we need to prevent systematic theology – and our own walk with God – from being dry, dusty, dangerous or divisive – because they in fact tend to foster faith, hope and love, our salvation and the glory of the God in whom we delight!

Questions for reflection or discussion

1 Before reading this introduction, what was your impression of 'theology'? What about 'systematic' theology?
2 Do we need systematic as well as biblical theology? What is the relationship between these two?
3 Which of the six theological keys in this book sounds most interesting to you?

---

22 Michael Horton, *Pilgrim Theology: Core Doctrines for Christian Disciples* (Grand Rapids: Zondervan, 2013).

1

God is not like us

If someone asked you, 'What is the Bible about?', what would you say?

As we've seen in the introduction, there are two ways we might begin to answer that question. We could start with the Bible's 'story', or we could start with the Bible's 'characters'. Where we actually begin our answer might depend on who asks us. In countries that have a long Christian heritage or tradition, it is usually possible to speak about 'God' and assume that most people know more or less whom we are talking about: the one, eternal, Creator God. If that knowledge can be assumed, we might get straight into the chronological story: *God created humans, but humans rebelled against God and incurred God's judgement, so God promised to send a Saviour,* and so on.

But in other contexts such an approach is less helpful – at least initially, perhaps. I'm a missionary in Japan, where there are, pro-verbially, eight million 'gods', none of whom is even remotely similar to the God of the Bible. To start speaking about 'God' to Japanese non-Christians, without explaining clearly who 'God' is, can cause great confusion. Increasingly, this is also the case when we speak to unchurched people in countries such as the UK and USA. Wherever we start, we ultimately need both 'story' and 'character' approaches. Introducing six theological keys to Scripture, this book focuses on the Bible's main 'characters': God and human beings.

The Bible is a book (or collection of sixty-six books) about God. True, God does not 'appear' in every book of the Bible. (He is not mentioned in Song of Solomon or Esther, although some biblical scholars have identified 'hints' of his presence in the text, and his presence is, we may take it, presumed by the authors of these books.)

But God is the main 'character' in the Bible, as well as its principal author.[1] The Bible begins and ends with God. That doesn't mean that the Bible is about nothing else. Such a claim would be manifestly false. Even a cursory glance at the Bible reveals that it is 'about' a whole range of things: families and nations, famines and wars, celebrations and calamities, heroes and villains. It contains a wide variety of literature, such as history, poetry, wisdom, prophecy and apocalyptic. But the Bible presents itself as – above all – the written Word of God: a true interpretation of reality, revealed by God to human beings, for a particular purpose.[2] As the fundamental or root reality, God himself is rightly at the centre of biblical revelation. Theologians are therefore correct to speak about God's 'self-revelation': *God reveals God.*

The question about how such revelation is possible (one aspect of the question of *knowledge*) is the subject of chapters 3 and 4 of this book. In this chapter (and the next) we'll be focusing on the question of *being* (ontology). In other words, we will be asking: *What* is God? and *Who* is God?

If God is the main 'character' in the Bible, the second most important 'character' is man.[3] Human beings are the secondary authors of almost every part of Scripture.[4] Of course, there are many different human characters in the Bible, from Adam and Eve, to Mary and Joseph, to Peter and Paul, and so on. But here we're concerned less with these characters as unique individuals, and more with what unites them to one another, and to *us*, as members of the same human race. Man was created as the crowning achievement

---

1 The Bible teaches its own divine authorship, or inspiration. Key texts that teach this doctrine are 2 Tim. 3:16 and 2 Peter 1:21. This divine authorship of Scripture does not compromise its human authorship.

2 We'll think about that purpose in chapters 5 and 6. For an excellent treatment of the doctrine of Scripture, or what the Bible teaches about itself, see John Frame, *The Doctrine of the Word of God* (Phillipsburg: P&R, 2010).

3 I will frequently use the masculine in this collective sense to mean 'all human beings'. I do not mean to exclude women: 'man' is often a more useful term. Unlike 'men and women' or 'human beings', the word 'man' can refer to either a plurality of people or a single person. For this reason 'man' corresponds best to its equivalent in Hebrew (*'ādām*), which is the original language of most of the Old Testament.

4 I say 'almost' because the Ten Commandments were originally, according to Exod. 31:18, 'written with the finger of God'.

of God's week of creation. Man's fall into sin and misery and the subsequent account of God's salvation of his people by the giving of his Son and Spirit is the principal 'melodic line' of Scripture's story. Above all, the single event at the centre of biblical (and world) history is the incarnation of the Son of God, when God assumed a human body and soul for ever in the man Jesus, who died, rose again and ascended on high. Man and God are now, literally, inseparable.

So, even if we were neither divine nor human[5] we would be unable to understand the Bible's story properly without a right understanding of both God *and* man, just as we noted from Calvin's famous words in the preface to this book.

In this chapter (and the next) we will therefore be asking – alongside our questions about God – the additional questions '*What* is man?' and '*Who* is man?'

Beginning with God: *What* or *who*?

Which is the right question to ask, '*What* is God?' or '*Who* is God?'?

Some theologians have argued that the question '**What** is God?' is illegitimate. Their reasoning is that God's essence (*what* he is) is beyond our ability to understand. Instead, we must focus our attention on the revealed personality of the God who has acted in history and given us an authoritative interpretation of his acts in the Bible. A further argument is that any human categories we might use to describe *what* God is are necessarily inappropriate and misleading – quite literally, 'category errors'. In other words, we should ask only '**Who** is God?'.

There is in fact much good sense in these arguments, and we'll return to issues of knowledge and understanding in chapter 3. But ultimately, I think we are wrong to reject entirely the question 'What is God?' for a couple of reasons.

First, and most importantly, in the Bible God *does* apparently tell us some things about *what* he is (e.g. God is love, God is spirit), and

---

5   For the sake of argument, we might be angels, for instance. We don't have too many more options besides being animals, plants or inanimate objects, and none of them need to worry about reading the Bible!

we need to take these seriously, allowing God himself to define what is meant by such descriptions.

Second, because God is unique (there is only one God), God's *essence* and God's *existence* necessarily coinhere: they are together as one. In other words, *who* God is and *what* God is can't ultimately be separated. In respect of human beings, that's obviously not the case. I am human, and so are you. We belong to the same genus (and species). But that doesn't mean we're the *same thing*. I am me and you are you. We can be in different places and do different things. We might not even know one another. For God, things are quite different. There is no genus called 'God' to which God belongs. Saying that 'God is God' is therefore, ultimately, the same as saying that 'God is'.[6] The God who *is* defines all categories of *what it is to be God* by his own being. Or, put another way, as soon as we start to talk about *who* God is, or what he is like, we at least begin to talk about *what* God is as well. But before we do either of these, we may begin by answering another, closely related, question: 'What is God **not**?'

One of the most basic truths that systematic theology teaches us about God is that *God is not like us*. It's the first of our six theological keys to Scripture. Actually, this is two truths in one: (1) God is not man, and (2) God is not *like* man. In beginning with negatives like this, I'm not suggesting that the most significant things we can say about God are negative.[7] Remember, this book is not about the six 'most significant' things the Bible says, but the six 'most basic' theological keys. These six keys are more like 'unbreakable rules' for interpretation than the 'last word' about the Bible or about God. It's your job as a believing Bible-reader to build on these foundations as

---

6 *Strictly speaking* according to etymology, God does not 'exist', because 'existence' is to have being 'out of' something else. God is the source of our being, and his life does not depend on anything or anyone else. However, this is probably a line of reasoning to avoid with our friends, given that we're very likely to be misunderstood if we say that God doesn't exist! Even many academic theologians will speak of the 'existence' of God without qualms.

7 Theologians call an approach that speaks of God in terms of negatives *apophatic* theology. Although apophatic theology is not the only appropriate way to do theology, I believe there is a place for it, especially when we express biblical rules or 'limits' on what theology can say. In addition, the Bible itself contains 'God is not . . .' statements, as we will see.

you go on to learn more and more about the God of the Bible and his gospel. You'll find many hints and pointers as we go on. But if you find yourself breaking (or, more likely, losing sight of) any of these rules, that's a sign you may be drifting away from what the Bible actually teaches.

There's a popular poster in the USA that reads, 'Two Basic Truths: There is a God and You Are Not He.'[8]

In the Bible, it is axiomatic (self-evident, basic and unquestionable) that *God is not man*. Indeed, God is not anything in creation. Theologians call this truth the *Creator–creature distinction*.

Less obvious, perhaps, is the truth that God is not *like* man. My children used to enjoy a game in which you compare totally unrelated things. 'Which do you prefer: pizza or air? Dad or Christmas?' It's fun to think about such comparisons, perhaps, but silly. The silliness depends on the category error. Pizza isn't really comparable with air, nor is Dad with Christmas. Now, if you *really* wanted to take the game seriously, you *could* find some things that pizza and air have in common. They're both made up of atoms and molecules, for instance – oxygen, carbon dioxide and nitrogen on the one hand, and cheese and tomato molecules (you can tell I'm a real scientist) on the other. Both pizza and air are *created*.

But you *can't* find things that God and man have in common, at least not *ontologically* speaking (in respect of *being*). Some theologians refer to this as the *infinite qualitative distinction* between God and man.[9] God is *infinitely* different from man, in every aspect of his being. When I first heard this idea, even as a Christian, it didn't sound right to me. Surely, I thought, there must be *something* that God and man have in common? What about when the Bible says that God is 'righteous' (Ps. 11:7) and Joseph is 'righteous' (Matt. 1:19, NRSV)? Doesn't that mean that God and Joseph share something (in this case, the property of being righteous)? Ontologically, the answer

---

8   This illustration is found in Michael Horton, *Pilgrim Theology: Core Doctrines for Christian Disciples* (Grand Rapids: Zondervan, 2013), 35.

9   The term 'infinite qualitative distinction' was first used by the Danish philosopher Søren Kierkegaard (1813–55), and later employed by the Swiss theologian Karl Barth (1886–1968). I'm using it in a slightly different way, following Reformed theologians like Cornelius Van Til (1895–1987).

is 'no'. God is in a class of his own. It's not just that his righteousness is much, much 'better' than Joseph's, or that God's righteousness is perfect while Joseph's is merely partial. God's righteousness is *infinitely* different from human righteousness, because God is infinite and we are not. Garry Williams puts it like this:

> God is beyond comparison with creation because he is the Creator, existing outside space and time in a way we cannot begin to imagine. His life and way of existing are different from ours and from everything else we know.[10]

So, this chapter is about the *Creator–creature distinction*, which I've further defined as the *infinite qualitative distinction* between God and man.

The story is told that twentieth-century philosopher-theologian Cornelius Van Til would begin his classes by drawing two circles on the board in his classroom, to depict the Christian world view.

Figure 1.1 **God and creation**

The top (larger) circle represents God. The bottom, smaller, circle represents creation, or everything else. Importantly, the circles do

---

10 Garry J. Williams, *His Love Endures for Ever: Reflections on the Love of God* (Nottingham: Inter-Varsity Press, 2015), 18.

not overlap at any point.[11] This is Van Til's way of depicting the *infinite qualitative distinction*.

But is this a *biblical* idea? Or is it something 'foreign' to the Bible, constructed by theologians who have moved away from the teaching of Scripture? We'll consider next – as we will in each subsequent chapter of this book – the biblical support for this theological key.

Biblical foundations

What support do we find in the Bible for our first theological key: *God is not like man*?

We can divide our answer into five parts or points:

1 The biblical teaching that God is *Creator* and man is *created* grounds the infinite qualitative distinction, as does the teaching that God is *Saviour* and man must *be saved*. Both truths underline the point that *God stands in a unique relation to creation*.
2 The revealed divine name 'I AM' distinguishes the being of God as being *from and of himself*, compared to man, whose being is always contingent and dependent.
3 The Bible repeatedly indicates things that only God can do (and man cannot do) or things that God cannot do (and man can or must do). Taken together, these descriptions enable us to build up an account of God's 'attributes' that distinguishes him as being utterly different from man.
4 The Bible sometimes speaks of God's nature *as God* in a way that distinguishes him from the essence of man, such as when it says that God is 'love', 'light' or 'spirit', compared to man. who is described as 'dust', 'flesh and blood', and so on.
5 The Bible teaches that God is simple and triune (three-in-one), whereas individual human beings are complex and unipersonal.

---

11 This story is found in John Frame, *Cornelius Van Til: An Analysis of His Thought* (Phillipsburg: P&R, 1995), 27. We will see in chapter 3 below how Van Til completed his diagram.

I've listed these five points in increasing order of conceptual difficulty, rather than logical priority or importance. The order here also reflects, roughly, the order in which these points come to our attention as we read through the Bible. Now, some theologians insist that the Trinity must be our starting point for everything we say about God. Indeed, this has been a popular position in twentieth- and twenty-first century theology. I certainly agree with such theologians that as Christian readers of the Bible we ought never to 'leave the Trinity behind' when we think about God. God is, and always has been, triune. We can't – or ought not to – somehow 'forget' that truth. But equally, it's clear that biblical revelation was given *incrementally* and *progressively*, over a period of 1,500 years. God's triunity was one of the last aspects of his being to be clearly revealed to us in Scripture. Most of the vocabulary we use to define what we mean by 'Trinity' comes from later centuries, and it arose in the process of the church reflecting on, and systematizing, biblical teaching to avoid false doctrine (heresy). So, although it's true that God is eternally triune, we don't need to find explicit (or even implicit) trinitarian doctrine in every passage of Scripture that talks about God, especially in the Old Testament. The Bible writers are often content to speak about 'God' when we now know that this means 'Father, Son and Holy Spirit'. We should not worry about doing this either, as long as our understanding of God continues to be informed by Scripture as we read and understand it with God's help. With that caveat in mind, let's consider each of the five points in a bit more detail.

1. First, we find that the Bible teaches the infinite qualitative distinction between God and man in the absolute difference between the uncreated Creator and his creation. There was a time when man was not. In contrast, there was never a time when God was not. The difference between created and uncreated being is therefore infinite. God has the attributes of **infinity** (he is without limit) and **eternity** (his infinity with respect to time), in stark contrast to human beings, and indeed everything else in all creation.

We find this right from the beginning of Scripture. Theologian John Murray writes, 'The data in Genesis 1:1 . . . are basic to all

Christian thought of God, of reality distinct from God, and of God's relation to this reality.'[12] Before God created the universe, there was nothing else (John 1:3). God created *ex nihilo* – Latin for 'from nothing'. In the creation account in Genesis 1:1 – 2:3, God created the heavens and the earth 'in the beginning', before man was created on the sixth day (1:1, 26–27). Psalm 90:2 says:

> Before the mountains were brought forth,
> or ever you had formed the earth and the world,
> *from everlasting to everlasting* you are God.
> (Emphasis added)

The Hebrew verb 'to create' (*bārā'*) is only ever used in the Bible with God as the subject. It is clear that the Bible points us to an incomparable Creator. In Isaiah 40, the prophet tells of the sovereign Creator's greatness, and of his utter difference from both the nations (man) and idols (false gods). He says in verse 18:

> To whom then will you liken God,
> or what likeness compare with him?

This is, of course, a rhetorical question. The only possible answer is 'no one'. When King David looked up to God's heavens, 'the work of your fingers, the moon and the stars, which you have set in place' (Ps. 8:3), he was moved to consider his own relative insignificance: '*What is man?*' (v. 4; emphasis added). In Psalm 102, God who is 'enthroned for ever' (v. 12) is contrasted with the human author, whose 'days pass away like smoke' (v. 3).

The infinite qualitative distinction is also established by God's being the Saviour, or Redeemer, of man.[13] The contrast here is that

---

12 John Murray, *Collected Writings*, 4 vols. (Edinburgh: Banner of Truth, 1977), 2:3.

13 It's no coincidence that Calvin structured his *Institutes* so that the first two books are called 'God the Creator' and 'God the Redeemer'. These 'acts' of creation and redemption are surely God's greatest in respect of the universe, and establish his relationship with creation as its 'Lord' twice over. As God reveals himself to us, we come to know him in both ways. More on this later.

man cannot save himself. Indeed, man must *be* saved (passive).[14] Creation and salvation are brought together in the poetry of Isaiah 45, where God declares to humankind (v. 22):

> Turn to me and be saved,
> all the ends of the earth!
> For I am God, and there is no other.

Only the true God can save. That is why it is folly to look for salvation anywhere (or in anyone) else, particularly in man:

> Put not your trust in princes,
>   in a son of man, in whom there is no salvation.
> When his breath departs, he returns to the earth;
>   on that very day his plans perish.
> Blessed is he whose help is the God of Jacob,
>   whose hope is in the LORD his God,
> who made heaven and earth,
>   the sea, and all that is in them,
> who keeps faith for ever;
>   who executes justice for the oppressed,
>   who gives food to the hungry.
> (Ps. 146:3–7)

The grounds of the psalmist's exhortation here to trust in the Lord are (1) God's eternity ('for ever'), (2) God's creating power and (3) God's saving power. In contrast, human beings (even the 'princes' among them) are mortal/finite, created and powerless to save.

2. We also see the infinite qualitative distinction hinted at in God's personal name. In Exodus 3:13, Moses asks God to reveal his name, and God replies, 'I AM WHO I AM' (v. 14). This cryptic Hebrew phrase becomes the basis for the personal name Yahweh, which in

---

14 That God is Saviour is a fitting and glorious expression of who he is. On the other hand I'm not suggesting that God is somehow 'constituted' by what he does in respect of creation. He would still be God without saving anyone. Again, I'll have more to say about this in chapter 6.

the Old Testament of most English Bibles is rendered 'the LORD' (in small capitals).[15] Much ink has been spilled on the meaning of this divine name, and theologians do not always agree on its precise significance. But it seems to me that this much is clear: it is a name that thoroughly distinguishes God from human beings. Man is always who God creates him to be. God defines man's existence. God, in contrast, is *who he is*. He defines himself, just as he gives life to himself. In the creation account, the first man 'names' the animals (Gen. 2:19). He even names his wife (Gen. 3:20)! But he cannot 'name' God. God names himself. God is in possession of what theologian John Webster refers to as 'matchless and utterly replete being in and from himself'.[16] This is sometimes referred to as God's **aseity** (or **independence**). It is the property of having self-existence, or life from oneself. Perhaps this is why in Scripture God is called nearly thirty times the 'living God'. Indeed, God cannot die: he is the 'immortal God' (Rom. 1:23).

In contrast, the Bible consistently describes human existence in quite different terms, as always and for ever contingent and dependent on God, who is the Giver of life. For example, in Acts 17:24–25, Paul tells the Athenians:

> The God who made the world and everything in it, being Lord of heaven and earth, does not live in temples made by man, nor is he served by human hands, as though he needed

---

15 We cannot be certain of the correct pronunciation of the Hebrew consonants YHWH. In existing manuscripts of the Old Testament, the vowel markings supplied are those for the generic word for 'Lord' (Adonai), rather than the word YHWH. This is because according to Jewish custom the name of God was not spoken when reading Scripture (for fear of taking it 'in vain' [Exod. 20:7]), but replaced by the generic term 'Adonai'. Over many centuries, absolute certainty about the original pronunciation was lost. As an aside, unless we're referring directly to Old Testament Scripture, there's no reason for us to write about 'the LORD' in capital letters in English. I can understand why some Christians might want to do that, but ultimately it's confusing because there's no 'underlying Hebrew' behind our English that we need to highlight, and both the Old Testament (partly) and the New Testament (completely) will happily refer to 'the Lord' (no capitals) when the underlying Hebrew text is not YHWH. Furthermore, if we're habitually going to write 'the LORD' in capitals, then why not 'GOD' as well, as in Isa. 26:4, and many other places in the Old Testament? We should aim for consistency as well as devotion in all of our God-talk!

16 John Webster, *God Without Measure: Working Papers in Christian Theology*, vol. 1: *God and the Works of God* (London: Bloomsbury T&T Clark, 2016), 16.

anything, since *he himself gives to all mankind life and breath and everything.*
(Emphasis added)

God gives life. Human life is therefore derivative, a divine gift.[17] This is not just a once-for-all derivation of life, but is continuous. After creating the world, God continues to preserve and govern the world – including human life – each moment of every hour. As Acts 17:25 suggests, every breath that we take is given to us by God. And in respect of *fallen* humanity, 'it is appointed for man to die' (Heb. 9:27).

One consequence of this absolute difference between the independent God and his dependent creation is that the relationship *creation* (including humanity) has with *God* must be very different from the relationship that *God* has with *creation*. In technical terms, the former relationship is called 'real' because creation's being is constituted by God and is for ever dependent upon God. But this sort of relationship cannot be mutual. The relationship God has with creation is therefore called 'rational', because God is neither constituted by, nor compromised by, creation.[18] God did not 'need' to create the world. Creation adds nothing to his being, just as it takes nothing away from him.

3. It is evident from Scripture that there are certain things only God can do, which man cannot do. Equally, there are some things that God cannot do, which man can do. Such contrasts support the theological key *God is not like us.* Indeed, sometimes these are specifically presented in the Bible as God–man contrasts. There are many possible examples I might cite of such contrasts, but below are a just a few:

'God is not man, that he should lie, / or a son of man, that he should change his mind. / Has he said, and will he not do it? / Or has he spoken,

17 See also 1 Tim. 6:13, where God is described as the one 'who gives life to all things'.

18 Theologians can say, on this basis, that God's relationship to creation is 'not real'. The potential for misunderstanding here (just as when theologians say that God does 'not exist') is significant, so it may well be better for most purposes to stick to explaining that God is never dependent or contingent on the world (unlike the other way round).

and will he not fulfil it?' (Num. 23:19). God cannot lie and cannot change his mind.[19] He fulfils every word he has spoken. In contrast, human beings can be (and often are) fickle and unfaithful (Rom. 3:13). A similar contrast is found in Malachi 3:6–7, where God first expresses his own immutable (unchanging) nature: 'I the LORD do not change'. This immutability is the basis for his people's security: 'therefore you, O children of Jacob, are not consumed'. Yet in contrast, the people themselves are quite different, since '[f]rom the days of [their] fathers [they] have turned aside from my statutes and have not kept them'.

'But will God indeed dwell with man on the earth? Behold, heaven and the highest heaven cannot contain you, how much less this house that I have built!' (2 Chr. 6:18). God cannot dwell on earth, or even in the 'highest heaven' (literally, the 'heaven of heavens') if this is understood to mean the created heavens. He certainly cannot dwell in a man-made 'house'.[20] In contrast, human beings are created to live on the earth, formed 'of dust from the ground' (Gen. 2:7).

Let no one say when he is tempted, 'I am being tempted by God', for God cannot be tempted with evil (Jas 1:13). God cannot be tempted. In contrast, man can be (and is) tempted (1 Cor. 10:13).

[H]e who does not love his brother whom he has seen cannot love God whom he has not seen (1 John 4:20). God is invisible (Col. 1:15; 1 Tim. 1:17). In contrast, man is visible, and visible *to God* even when he attempts to hide, because God is everywhere (Ps. 139:7–12; Prov. 15:3).

'And do not fear those who kill the body but cannot kill the soul. Rather fear him who can destroy both soul and body in hell' (Matt. 10:28). As Jesus teaches here, God has power over the eternal destiny of

---

19 I'm aware of passages of the Bible that say that God 'changed his mind' or 'repented'. We'll come back to the issues raised by these texts later on.

20 Heb. 9:9, 11 indicates that the 'dwelling' of God in the tabernacle (and presumably later in the temple) was 'symbolic' (literally, a 'parable') of 'the greater and more perfect tent (not made with hands, that is, not of this creation)', which is to be found in the uncreated heaven, or eternal dwelling place of God.

human beings. In contrast, the most or worst man can do is destroy physical life.

'[T]he Lord sees not as man sees: man looks on the outward appearance, but the Lord looks on the heart' (1 Sam. 16:7). God 'looks' beneath the surface, even to the inner workings of the human heart. In contrast, man is limited to what he can see on the outside.

As I've said, there are many more examples in the Bible of things that only God (not man or other creatures) can do or be. In fact, strictly speaking every attribute of God is unique to God. Even those attributes that are often called 'communicable' (such as knowledge, power, love and righteousness), because God can 'communicate' them to human beings, are attributed to God in an infinite and eternal sense, which sets them apart. So God does not merely 'know': he is *omni*-scient (knowing all things). He is not merely 'powerful': he is *omni*-potent (all-powerful). Even his love and righteousness are infinitely different from ours.[21] In addition, as we'll see in a moment, God's attributes can't be thought of as 'add-ons' to God's being. They *are* his being.

One other teaching of the Bible about God that sets him apart from us is that he is **unchanging** or **immutable**. We've seen this attribute hinted at in some of the Bible passages above. With God, James tells us, 'there is no variation or shadow due to change' (Jas 1:17). Whatever this means, it cannot mean that God is somehow inert or emotionless. That would be to contradict other parts of Scripture, which we'll consider in the next chapter. But equally, we cannot ignore the Bible's testimony to God's unchanging nature. It's why God is also often described by theologians as **impassible** (unable to be acted upon, or to suffer). Again, we must not try to interpret this attribute according to purely human categories. A human being who was impassible would be entirely incapable of relationship! That

---

21 Donald Macleod has argued that the traditional distinction between incommunicable and communicable attributes is not sustainable, because there are *no* attributes of God that are communicable to creatures in precisely the way they are attributed to God. See Donald Macleod, *Behold Your God* (Fearn: Christian Focus, 1995), 20–21.

is quite unlike God, who is both fully relational and the ground of all our relationships (Eph. 3:14–15). But we must take seriously the biblical witness to God's unchanging nature, which is never as it were 'acted upon' by outside forces that take him by surprise.

4. Attentive readers of the Bible will know that there are times when Scripture tells us 'God is . . . + substantive (noun)' in such a way that the text seems to make a straightforward claim about God's essence or his being. The three most famous examples of this – all from the writings of the apostle John – are: 'God is spirit' (John 4:24), 'God is light' (1 John 1:5), and 'God is love' (1 John 4:8).[22] It's not our purpose here to unpack the full meaning of these statements. They are hardly to be thought of as 'definitions' of God. But I want you to notice that at least one implication of such descriptive terms is to 'mark off' God *as God*, distinguishing him and setting him apart from human beings.

Biblically speaking, man is not 'spirit' in the way that God is 'spirit'. To be sure, man *has* a spirit, and this spirit is formed by and given to him by God (Zech. 12:1). But man is also 'flesh and blood'.[23] In another idiom, man is but 'dust', into which God breathes life.[24] To go a step further, man is, biblically, a psychosomatic[25] union: a created combination of soul (or spirit) and flesh-and-bone, 'dusty' body.[26] When we die, our 'dust returns to the earth as it was, and [our] spirit returns to God who gave it' (Eccl. 12:7). At least temporarily, we'll have an existence according to which our bodies will be separated from our spirits. But the Bible insists that this is a temporary, unnatural existence. We are destined for resurrection: the reunification of spirit and body (1 Cor. 15:50–54). Paul does say that 'flesh and blood cannot inherit the kingdom of God' (v. 50). Our

---

22 Often overlooked, probably because the grammatical forms are different, are the comparable expressions in Mark 14:62, which (though lacking the copula) calls God the 'Power', and Isa. 6:3, which (though adjectival) may be understood essentially: God is holiness 'through and through'.

23 Matt. 16:17; 1 Cor. 15:50; Eph. 6:12; Heb. 2:14. In the Old Testament in particular, there are many references to 'all flesh' that probably refer in the main to human beings.

24 Gen. 2:7; Job 34:15; Ps. 90:3; 1 Cor. 15:49. On the 'breath of life' see Gen. 2:7.

25 From the Greek *psychē* (soul) and *sōma* (body).

26 I find 'dichotomous' (two-part) accounts of man more persuasive biblically than 'trichotomous' (three-part) accounts, which press a distinction between the human 'soul' and 'spirit'. But a full discussion is beyond the scope of this book.

resurrection bodies will not be of the 'dust'. But they will be *bodies*, and it is in those bodies that we'll spend an everlasting future, whether in God's gracious presence, or shut out from it.

God, on the other hand, *is* spirit, and his **spirituality** goes hand in hand with his inherent **invisibility**.[27] God has no body. To say that God is 'spirit' is not to refer to the Holy Spirit. (We'll return to him in the next subsection.) God's spirituality means that he is *pure spiritual being*. He has none of the properties of matter. You cannot measure God in any way – theologians call this God's **immensity**. God cannot be weighed, or sized up, or have his temperature taken. Rather, everything else that *is*, is measured by God's standards.

Note that to say that 'God is light' is not the same as to say that 'light is God'. We cannot simply reverse statements like this. Yet there is a sense in which *true* light *is* God. He alone is *uncreated light*. God therefore defines light by his being. He is '[t]he true light, which enlightens everyone' (John 1:9). Biblically, visions of God or of his 'glory' may be accompanied by light, even 'blinding' light. (Think of Saul/Paul in Acts 9, who saw a 'light from heaven' [v. 3] that left him blind.) God is light. But God is also the one who *creates* light, his first creative act in Scripture (Gen. 1:3). Every other source of light in creation is derivative, *created* light, including of course 'the greater light to rule the day and the lesser light to rule the night' (Gen. 1:16). The sun and moon were commonly worshipped in ancient pagan religions, but in the Bible even these heavenly lights are relativized because they are *created*. Once again, human beings cannot be 'light' in the way that God is light. God may 'enlighten' us (Ps. 19:8; Heb. 6:4). He can 'give' light to us (Ps. 119:130; John 1:9, NIV). We may even receive 'the light of life' (Ps. 56:13; John 8:12), just as we receive a spirit from him. But this light does not come from ourselves. Always and for ever we must confess to God that:

> with you is the fountain of life;
> in your light do we see light.
> (Ps. 36:9)

---

27 On the invisibility of God, we've already noted above Col. 1:15 and 1 Tim. 1:17.

'God is love' is another biblical statement that must be rightly interpreted, according to the theological key *God is not like man*. In his excellent book on the love of God, Garry Williams perceptively points out that 'love' is the attribute of God we may be most likely to misunderstand, given our tendency to interpret 'love' in human categories.[28] We need to understand God's love *for us* in the way that he has revealed it to us in Scripture, not (first) according to our experiences, or by the standards of imperfect human love. Once again, our love for God, or for others, is always derivative of his perfect love: 'We love because he first loved us' (1 John 4:19). Even when our love is by God's grace 'perfected' (1 John 2:5; 4:12, 17–18) as it one day will be, it will never be qualitatively the same as God's love.

But God's love *for us* is not the only divine love the Bible tells us about. We also learn that God is love *in himself,* apart from the existence of a created universe as the object of his love. We'll think more about this in the next subsection, but the reason this is possible is because the Bible tells us that God is a trinity of divine 'Persons' – Father, Son and Holy Spirit. The Father loves the Son (John 3:35). The Son loves the Father (John 14:31). The Holy Spirit – we may assume – also participates in this love, so much so that, following a tradition established by St Augustine in the fifth century, the Spirit has been described as the 'bond of love' between the Father and the Son.[29] As Williams puts it, '[i]t is this trinitarian love that is the first love, an eternal love that stands before all other loves. This is the love that defines all other loves.'[30] At the same time, '[h]uman love is appropriately *different* from God's love, because it is human and not divine'.[31] Once again, the infinite

---

28 Williams, *His Love Endures for Ever*, 26.

29 Is there biblical support for such a description of the Holy Spirit? Not directly so, but the Spirit is described in a number of texts as the gracious or good 'gift' of God (Luke 11:13; Acts 2:38; 10:45; by extension, Heb. 6:4). The Spirit is also the Person of the Trinity particularly associated with 'fellowship' (2 Cor. 13:14), which fellowship is loving relationship with the Father and the Son (1 John 1:3). It is not too much of a stretch to speak of the Holy Spirit as the intratrinitarian 'bond of love', as long as we remember that this is not everything that may be said about him, and as long as we keep in mind that he is a 'Person' rather than an impersonal force or power.

30 Williams, *His Love Endures for Ever*, 46.

31 Ibid. 40.

qualitative distinction between God and man must not be forgotten. *God is not like us!*

5. The Bible teaches that God is simple and triune (three-in-one). God is one essence and three Persons. 'Essence' and 'Person' are not biblical terms when used in this sense, but they are the best words we have to articulate the oneness and threeness of God. The Father is God, the Son is God and the Spirit is God. And they are three distinct Persons. And there is one God, who is a 'personal' God. Again, the purpose of this book is not to offer a complete introduction to theology, so I'm not going to go through all of the biblical support for the doctrine of the Trinity, which you can find in an introductory textbook.[32] Nor am I going to try to defend the doctrine of the Trinity logically or philosophically.[33] Rather, my more limited purpose here is to demonstrate that *God is not like man*.

The first way in which this is so is that man is *complex*, not *simple*. To say that man is 'complex' means that you can divide him up into his constituent 'parts'. You can, should you so choose, take a human being to pieces. We know this is possible: some of us will have signed a pledge to donate our bodies to medical science or our organs to those who need them after our death. Or, you might (if you could) remove a single human attribute from an individual, and that individual would still remain human. If I lost all my (sadly mediocre) 'golfing ability', perhaps because I lost my arms in an accident, I would still be a human being. Indeed, I would still be me. Likewise, you can add attributes: a human being can learn new things, develop and change. This is why we say that man is *complex*.

God, on the other hand, has the attribute of **simplicity**. This doesn't mean he is easy to understand. It means he cannot be divided up. Chapter 2 of the *Westminster Confession of Faith* says that God is 'without body, parts, or passions'.[34] One necessary implication of

---

32 See e.g. ch. 4 of Horton, *Pilgrim Theology*.
33 I'm not sure that I could, although others have tried. I tend towards thinking that the idea of trinity, while not strictly *illogical*, *transcends* human logic. More on this in the chapters on knowledge (3 and 4) to come.
34 Here the confession echoes the first of the Church of England's thirty-nine 'Articles of Religion'. The particular phrase goes back to the forty-two articles of 1553.

God's simplicity is that no one, single attribute of God can be 'more' definitive of God than any other. He *is* his attributes, just as he is *all* his attributes, and each attribute may be rightly understood only in the light of the rest. In other words, God is always, equally and maximally, powerful, wise, holy, free and absolute, just as he is always, equally and maximally, glorious, loving, gracious, merciful, long-suffering, good and true – and this is by no means an exhaustive list of God's biblical attributes. Another implication of God's simplicity is that we cannot 'separate' or 'extract' God's will or his knowledge from God. Just as God *is* uncreated light, and God *is* love, God *is* (his) will. God *is* (his) knowledge. All of this is so manifestly different from man!

Second, man is not trinitarian. In contrast to God, individual human beings are unipersonal. There is no distinction between 'persons' in a human being. I can love myself (Eph. 5:28) but only because I have a body to love, in other words, because I am complex. I have no ability to fellowship with myself. I am made for community, and – as the 2020 coronavirus lockdown has demonstrated – if I spend too long alone, I will come to long for company with others. In this respect, again, I'm infinitely unlike God, who doesn't know loneliness or need, but always (for eternity) has enjoyed maximal bliss in himself, quite apart from the creation of the universe, or fellowship with creatures.

As I've noted above, the doctrines of God's simplicity and (particularly) his triunity have been denied by various heretical groups in church history, usually as a result of a failure to interpret Scripture rightly, according to Scripture's own rules for interpretation. What is at the root of this? God, says theologian J. I. Packer, is the 'incomparable one'.[35] That has been the central theological key at the heart of this chapter: *God is not like us*. Nevertheless, it is always our (sinful) human tendency to compare him to ourselves. In Packer's words, 'We think of God as too much like what we are.'[36]

---

35 J. I. Packer, *Knowing God*, 2nd edn (London: Hodder & Stoughton, 1993; first publ. 1973), 96.
36 Ibid. 93.

Implications of the theological key

The implications of the theological key *God is not like us* are both doctrinal and practical. In both areas we need to maintain a radical commitment to the utter *otherness* of God.

Such a commitment ensures that we do not read the Bible in a *pantheist* way. **Pantheism** is the belief that everything is divine. More subtle, perhaps, is the idea of **panentheism**. According to panentheism, there is a mutual dependence between 'God' and the world, so that the universe is somehow *in* God.[37] Cornelius Van Til, whose two-circle diagram of the Christian world view we've already encountered above, would represent the non-Christian world view with a single circle. In pantheism and panentheism, 'God' and everything else are ultimately part of the same 'stuff'. As we've seen, neither of these world views is compatible with the biblical account of God and his relationship to creation.

Another world view ruled out of court by the infinite qualitative distinction is **polytheism**. This was the prevalent world view in the ancient Near East (the biblical world), just as it is the prevalent world view in Japan, where I serve as a missionary. In Japanese Shinto, there *is* an idea of a 'creator' god, called Amaterasuomikami.[38] But Amaterasuomikami is ultimately part of the same 'stuff' as creation itself, just as are all the other 'gods'. In the past, I had a friendship with a Shinto priest who was a visiting student in Oxford, where I was a pastor. We met regularly over the period of a year or so to study the Bible and to talk about Shinto. By the end of the year, this Shinto priest had accepted that Jesus Christ was both his Creator and his Saviour! However, he could not accept the idea that the gods of Shinto were idols, to be rejected. Instead, he argued that Jesus was the Creator of the Shinto gods, and he felt vindicated *by Jesus* to

---

37 On panentheism, see John M. Frame, *A History of Western Philosophy and Theology* (Phillipsburg: P&R, 2015), 445.

38 Shinto is the traditional, animistic religion of Japan, often combined in the popular mind with varieties of Buddhism. Many Japanese will say that Shinto is not a 'religion'. Of course, that depends on the definition of 'religion', but to my mind Shinto combines explanatory power with psychological and visceral demands for commitment, which features make it 'religious'.

continue in his vocation as a Shinto priest. What was behind this? We might suppose that he was simply rejecting Scripture's clear teaching, even though I explained it to him as clearly as I could. But at a deep level of understanding (whether intentionally or not) I think my friend never got to grips with the infinite qualitative distinction. For him, God and the gods were all on a sort of continuum, with human beings somewhere on the same continuum. Everything, in his view, shared the common property of being, in the same way. His polytheism was, in the end, a version of panentheism.

Many Christian Bible readers may instinctively reject pantheism and panentheism, without thinking too much about these world views. However, we should always be aware of the danger of such non-Christian approaches infiltrating our theologies. Any time we think of God as in any way 'dependent' on, or 'needing', the world, we are heading in a panentheist direction. When we start to think that God changes in his essence (or his attributes, which are equal to his essence, on the principle of divine simplicity), we similarly invite a panentheist perspective into our theology. On the other hand, if we insist that God's simplicity rules out *any* distinction of personality (or diversity within unity), we may tend towards Islam's understanding of Allah. It is difficult on this basis for Muslims to speak of God as 'love', for if he loves apart from the world, whom does he love?

Some of the attributes of God have been challenged in different ways by theologians in recent years, occasionally by theologians from evangelical backgrounds or those who share many other evangelical commitments. For example, so-called Open Theists deny God's immutability and impassibility, as well as his omniscience, at least as traditionally understood.[39] This is not the place to enter into all the discussions. But ultimately, any theology that denies one or more of these incommunicable attributes of God has likely forgotten (or rejected) in some way the theological key *God is not like us.*

---

39 In 2001, the Evangelical Theological Society voted to reject Open Theism as an acceptable option for evangelicals, releasing a statement on God's omniscience. Immutability and (particularly) impassibility remain somewhat controversial.

Without this theological key as a foundation for our Bible-reading, we are likely to be led astray by overemphasizing passages that speak of God's 'changing' in some way. (More on this later.) A misstep at this point robs us of the comfort that God's utter difference affords. As John Owen wrote, 'That the Lord often establishe[s] his saints in the assurance of the unchangeableness of his love towards them from the immutability of his own nature is very evident.'[40]

One important area of biblical understanding where this first theological key comes into its own is the question 'Who is Jesus?'[41] The Bible teaches us that Jesus is both God and man. Theologians say that he has two 'natures'. The divine and human natures of Jesus don't mix together to become something else. They remain distinct, even though they have come together for ever in one 'person' (another technical term in theology). When we read about Jesus Christ in the Bible, then, we need to keep in mind that he is *both* the God who is infinitely distinct from the world, *and* at the same time he is fully man. Christ's two natures – divine and human – are both distinct and united in the one Person. How can this possibly be? The 'incarnation' (the event in which the eternal Son of God takes a human nature) is full of mystery, and this book will not offer a complete treatment of the subject.[42] But the idea that Jesus has two natures can partly be expressed by means of the biblical concept of Jesus as the 'image' of God. We'll return to that in the next chapter. I'll also have a bit more to say about the incarnation in the final chapter, when we look at God's saving acts.

Insisting on the Creator–creature distinction has implications for our **worship** of God. It is right that God deserves our absolute service and devotion, because he is infinitely different from us. This is the consistent picture of God that we receive in Scripture. Consider David's prayer in 1 Chronicles 29:11:

---

40 John Owen, *The Doctrine of the Saints' Perseverance Explained and Confirmed*, in *The Works of John Owen*, 16 vols. (Banner of Truth: Edinburgh, 1965), 11:130.

41 This book began with a related question: Where is Jesus? We'll return to that question at the end of the book.

42 We should not imagine that Jesus' human nature was personal in itself, as though in Christ God is united to some pre-existing human being. Rather, in the incarnation Christ's human nature is 'personalized' by virtue of being united to the eternal Word of God. Christ is therefore fully man as well as fully God.

Yours, O LORD, is the greatness and the power and the glory
and the victory and the majesty, for all that is in the heavens
and in the earth is yours. Yours is the kingdom, O LORD, and
you are exalted as head above all.

God is ultimate. So he is worthy of all honour. Indeed, this is why he
has made us – for his own glory (Isa. 43:7). As C. S. Lewis has
suggested, it goes with the grain of our being to worship someone
who is infinitely worthy of our praise. God is so much the fundamental reality that to know him 'is simply to be awake, to have
entered the real world', and not to appreciate him 'is to have lost the
greatest experience, and in the end to have lost all'.[43]

There are also implications for our **self-understanding** and **moral
worth** as human beings. It's no bad thing to be finite. It's a good
thing that we're not God! We don't have overall responsibility for the
universe. As Horton says, we have 'the gift of a distinct, creaturely
existence'.[44] To recognize this truth is not to shirk or dodge creaturely
responsibility. Rather, God's aseity grounds our creaturely existence,
and is the context for the responsibility that we owe to our Creator.
In addition, a right view of God's utter transcendence should make
us both humble and concerned for others. As Kelly M. Kapic writes,
'Pride has lost sight of the gap between the holy Creator and sinful
humanity, producing self-absorption and contempt for others.'[45]
Here again we can see the fundamental connection between our
knowledge of God and our knowledge of ourselves.

Recognizing that *God is not like man* is one of the grounds of our
salvation. It is precisely because God is not part of the world, and
not creaturely or finite, that he is able to save us. The divine attributes
of omnipotence, omniscience, omnipresence, immutability and
impassibility are all crucial in this regard. We can *really trust* that
God will do as he has promised, because he is almighty, and does
not change.

---

43 C. S. Lewis, *Reflections on the Psalms* (1st edn, 1958; repr., New York: Harcourt, Brace,
Jovanovich, 1986), 92.
44 Horton, *Pilgrim Theology*, 36.
45 Kelly M. Kapic, *A Little Book for New Theologians: How and Why to Study Theology*
(Downers Grove: InterVarsity Press, 2012), 71.

Finally, this also has implications on a day-to-day basis for our **prayer** lives. Because God is not contained in or by the universe, we can bring our requests to him with confidence in his utter sovereign power to act according to his will. He is never constrained, except by himself. Praying through the sublime collection of prayers in *The Valley of Vision*, it is striking how often categories of *systematic* theology inform both devotion and supplication. For example:

> O God most high, most glorious,
> The thought of thine infinite serenity cheers me,
> For I am toiling and moiling, troubled and distressed,
>   but thou art for ever at perfect peace.[46]

Prayers such as this one reflect our experience as well as our faith. That's why, on one level at least, believers are perhaps unlikely to reckon that we are like God. Certainly, few Bible-readers would think of themselves as 'divine': fewer still would publicly *admit* to such an out-and-out blasphemy! But there remains a powerful temptation to think of God in human terms. It is far too easy for us to try to bring God down to our own level. The infinite qualitative distinction helps guard against this. However we think of God, however we describe him, however we relate to him, however we teach about him, we should be careful to insist that *God is not like us*.[47] As theologian Herman Bavinck put it more than a century ago, 'The distance between God and us is the gulf between the Infinite

---

46 Arthur Bennett (ed.), *The Valley of Vision: A Collection of Puritan Prayers and Devotions* (Edinburgh: Banner of Truth, 1975), 127.

47 How should we teach this biblical truth to children? When I taught Sunday school for two-to four-year-olds for a couple of years, one of the songs we most often sang was 'Our God Is a Great Big God' (2001, Vineyard Songs). The lyrics say (among other things) that God is 'higher than a skyscraper', 'deeper than a submarine', and 'wider than the universe'. One potential problem with such comparisons is that they tend to suggest that God is just higher, deeper and wider than some other big things that children are familiar with. If we do use such comparisons with our children, we should try to show them that God is *utterly* and *infinitely* different. Admittedly, that is a difficult idea. In fairness to the song 'Our God Is a Great Big God', it does attempt to communicate such a difference, making an appeal to eternity ('before the world began') and insisting that God is 'beyond my wildest dreams'. Paul's prayer in Eph. 3:14–19 similarly links the spatial language of 'breadth and length and height and depth' with the knowledge of that which ultimately 'surpasses knowledge'. We'll return to these verses in Ephesians in chapter 4.

and the finite, between eternity and time, between being and becoming, between the All and the nothing.'[48] This is the God who encounters us in Scripture, and in the majestic universe he has created. Fear and trembling ought to be our first response! In Donald Macleod's words, '[t]heology has lost its way, and, indeed its very soul, if it cannot say with John, 'I fell at his feet as dead' (Rev. 1:17).'[49]

> Thou eternal God,
> Thine is surpassing greatness, unspeakable goodness,
>   super-abundant grace;
> I can as soon count the sands of ocean's 'lip' as number
>   thy favours towards me;
> I know but a part, but that part exceeds all praise.[50]

Questions for reflection or discussion

1 What is the 'infinite qualitative distinction' between God and man?
2 What attributes of God set him apart as being utterly different from us?
3 How might understanding the theological key *God is not like us* help you in your reading of the Bible? What about in your Christian life?

---

48 Herman Bavinck, *Reformed Dogmatics*, vol. 2: *God and Creation*, edited by John Bolt, translated by John Vriend (Grand Rapids: Baker Academic, 2004), 30.
49 Macleod, *Behold Your God*, 39.
50 Bennett, *Valley of Vision*, 10.

2

God has made us like himself

I wonder how you felt at the end of the last chapter? Perhaps it seemed to you that the God I described there – infinitely different from us in every respect – isn't the God that you know from the Bible and from your experience? Maybe you felt like you were only getting part of the picture?

With the theological key *God is not like us* I stressed the *otherness* of God in order to highlight the Bible's identification of God as the one who is *utterly transcendent and distinct from his creation*. I hope you were able to see that this is indeed an important aspect of what the Bible teaches about who God is. This theological key ought to affect the way we live, worship, pray, evangelize and of course how we interpret Scripture. God is always the Transcendent One, or, to borrow Michael Horton's term, 'The Stranger'.

But if you felt like you were only getting half the picture in the last chapter, you'd be quite right. God's transcendence relative to his creation is not the whole story. In this chapter, we're going to consider the other side of the dialectic, with the theological key *God has made us like himself*. Remember that *dialectic* means a way of discovering what is true by considering opposites. In the case of the theological keys introduced in this book, 'opposites' is maybe not the best description. Each pair of theological keys sets up an apparent contrast. They are not contradictions or paradoxes, but 'antinomies' (J. I. Packer's word) and the full truth of both keys must be maintained if we are to understand the Bible faithfully.[1] So, *God is not like*

---

1 J. I. Packer explains that a paradox is, strictly, 'a form of statement that seems to unite two opposite ideas, or to deny something by the very terms in which it is asserted'. What is significant about a paradox is that the appearance of contradiction is *verbal*, rather than *factual*. An example is Paul's description of himself in 2 Cor. 6:10 as 'having nothing, yet possessing everything'. A paradox, then, is 'always dispensable' and 'always

us. Period.[2] But also, and at the same time, *God has made us like himself.* This is why Horton can say that God is the Stranger we meet.[3]

In this chapter, then, we'll see that the God of the Bible is *immanent* as well as *transcendent*. He is the God who says:

> I dwell in the high and holy place,
> *and also* with him who is of a contrite and lowly spirit . . .
> (Isa. 57:15; emphasis added)

We'll see, further, that man is introduced to us in the Bible as a created being who is made *as the likeness* of God. Of course, we'll have to consider exactly what this means, paying close attention to the biblical data. But perhaps we can sense already that this chapter will take us in a profoundly different direction from the previous one. In the last chapter, we followed the biblical descriptions of God and man to separate them as far as possible in terms of being. We were quite right to do that. The Bible clearly teaches such an understanding. But in this chapter, in contrast, we'll trace the Bible's testimony to the *closeness* between God and man. Does that sound 'surprising?' I hope it does. I think we're meant to feel the surprise – even the amazement. It's never to be taken for granted that God should have a close relationship with any of his creatures, formed from the dust. So, with heads bowed low, and hearts appropriately humbled, let's consider our next theological key: *God has made us like himself.*

---

comprehensible'. Paul could have explained in what sense he means that he has nothing, and in what (different) sense he means that he possesses everything, and we could have understood him plainly. In contrast, what Packer calls an 'antinomy' is 'unavoidable' and 'insoluble'. We must not try to (because we cannot, at least not fully) 'explain' the antinomy. Rather, we must assert both ideas. Each pair of theological keys in this book is an antinomy, in the sense that Packer uses the term. See J. I. Packer, *Divine Sovereignty and Human Responsibility: How Both Biblical Truths Coexist in God's Grace* (1961), <https://www.gracegems.org/30/packer_divine_sovereignty.htm>. Accessed 19 June 2019.

2 Or 'full stop', as we say in Great Britain.
3 Michael Horton, *Pilgrim Theology: Core Doctrines for Christian Disciples* (Grand Rapids: Zondervan, 2013), 35.

Man: the image of God

You *are* the image of God. This is the most profound and basic answer to the great question 'Who am I?', which is a question about being.

Furthermore, **you are *to be* the image of God.** This is the answer to another great question, 'How shall I live?', which is a question about acting, or ethics.

It is hard to overestimate the importance of this biblical concept, both for our identity and for our calling as human beings. Biblically, the image of God is both a definition *of* man and a vocation *for* man. It is something we *are*, and also something we – in Christ – *become*.

In this book, we're going to follow these two senses of the 'image of God' in different chapters. Here we're interested in *being*. So our focus will be on what is called the 'wider' sense of the image of God.[4] In chapter 5 we'll return to the 'narrower' sense.[5]

So what does it mean to say that man is the image of God? Many interesting suggestions have been made. Rather than work through all the options, I want to make the case for the option that I find most satisfying.

In the Bible, we begin with the familiar words of Genesis 1:26–27:

> Then God said, 'Let us make man in our image, after our likeness. And let them have dominion over the fish of the sea and over the birds of the heavens and over the livestock and over all the earth and over every creeping thing that creeps on the earth.'

> So God created man in his own image,
>   in the image of God he created him;
>   male and female he created them.

---

4 This is sometimes called the 'essential' or 'metaphysical' sense of the image.
5 This is sometimes called the 'accidental' or 'ethical' sense.

In the story of creation, man is created along with the animals on the sixth day. In some respects, then, man is like the animals. He is given a similar kind of blessing to the blessing received by the fish and the birds (compare v. 22 with v. 28). He gets the same food to eat as the animals (v. 29). He is pronounced 'good', just as the other animals and birds are (vv. 25, 31).

But in one – most important – respect, man is *different* from the animals, and indeed from every other part of creation. The theological key for this chapter is, remember, *God has made us like himself.* Biblically, this is expressed in the language of the 'image' and 'likeness' of God. What does this mean? You may have noticed that I began this section by saying that man *is* the image of God. Many of us, probably, are used to thinking that man is made 'in' the image of God: after all, that's what most English Bible translations say. Perhaps you've been told that it means man shares some characteristics with God, such as rationality, spirituality, freedom of choice, the ability to love, and so on. Well, I think we *do* 'share' certain things with God (although in a particular, qualified, way, given the infinite qualitative distinction we looked at in the last chapter). But I don't think that's (first and foremost) what it means to be God's 'image'.

The Hebrew words for 'image' and 'likeness' in Genesis 1[6] have a specific and widely recognized meaning in the ancient world and in cognate (related) languages in particular. This meaning can be either religious or political. In (pagan) religious terms, both words typically refer to an 'idol', in the concrete sense of *the cult statue of a god*. In political terms, they refer to *statues of kings*, or else to *kings themselves as living 'images' of the gods.*[7]

With this background in mind, we may note that it is entirely possible (grammatically) to translate the prepositions 'in' and 'according to' in Genesis 1:26–27 (ESV) as 'as'.[8] Although God speaks

---

6 These are *ṣelem* (usually translated 'image') and *děmût* (usually translated 'likeness').
7 In our modern world, we separate the 'religious' from the 'political' much more than in the ancient world, where they were closely linked, as this set of meanings reveals.
8 Hebrew *beth* and *kaph*. There are other biblical examples of this usage of beth (the so-called beth of identity), in which something earthly is said to represent a heavenly original. *Kaph* is not well attested in this sense, but the meaning is certainly not impossible. It is true that

in the plural in verse 26 (just as he does in some other places in the Old Testament) it is most likely he is referring to *himself* rather than including angels or other heavenly beings in the concept of the image. No other passage in either testament of the Bible compels us to think that the image refers to something other than God on the one hand, or else is limited to an aspect of man's being on the other hand.[9] In fact, there is a simple equation: Man *is* the image of God, and the image is of *God*.[10]

Jeffrey J. Niehaus has helped us to understand this concept in its ancient Near Eastern context.[11] As we might expect from the linguistic data above, the idea has both religious and political echoes. According to Niehaus, pagan religion typically taught that a god would reveal his or her 'presence' or 'face'[12] to the worshipper by means of an idol. On the basis of his research Niehaus says, '[t]he idol (or 'image' or 'likeness' in ancient Near Eastern parlance) not only *represented* the god, but, it was thought, also *embodied* the god'.[13] Niehaus gives examples from ancient Egypt and concludes that 'in Egypt an idol ... was made to represent a heavenly archetype

---

(note 8 *cont.*) both are translated with the Greek *kata* in the Septuagint (Old Testament in Greek) and this is the usual wording we find in the New Testament (as in e.g. Jas 3:9, although note the exception in 1 Cor. 11:7). *Kata* is usually rendered in English as 'in', or 'according to'. However, the authoritative Greek New Testament lexicon (dictionary) – usually known as 'BDAG' after the initials of its authors and revisors – classifies the use of *kata* in Jas 3:9 as 'a periphrasis to express equality, similarity, or example in accordance with'. Furthermore, BDAG includes Eph. 4:24 and Col. 3:10 (both passages where the 'renewal' of the image of God is being discussed) as examples of the same use of *kata*. There would therefore seem to be strong support for translating *kata* as 'as' in these verses.

9 1 Cor. 15:49, by its use of the verb *phoreō* (to bear), does seem to suggest that an image (in this case that of the man of dust, Adam, and that of the heavenly man, Christ) is something *extrinsic* to (outside) man. But even with this use of 'bearing' language the question of the relationship between the man and the image is not resolved. BDAG notes that the use of *phoreō* here is figurative, and means 'to identify habitually with something'. Such idiomatic use of *phoreō* is especially common in the sense of 'bearing a name', which in biblical contexts often implies the closest possible identification (even of being/ontology) with the person of that name. We may conclude that there is no biblical text that invalidates the case presented here that *man is the image of God*.

10 Herman Bavinck also defended the position that 'a human being does not *bear* or *have* the image of God but that he or she *is* the image of God' (emphases original). Herman Bavinck, *Reformed Dogmatics*, vol. 2: *God and Creation*, edited by John Bolt, translated by John Vriend (Grand Rapids: Baker Academic, 2004), 554.

11 Jeffrey J. Niehaus, *Ancient Near Eastern Themes in Biblical Theology* (Grand Rapids: Kregel, 2008).

12 These are the same words in biblical Hebrew and many other ancient languages.

13 Ibid. 99. Emphases mine.

[original]'.[14] The god was considered to be present in his image. In addition, an early pyramid text describes the king of Egypt (Pharaoh) as 'the most sacred of the sacred images of the Great One' (the creator).[15] It's clear that in Egypt, the king himself was thought to be the 'image' of a god. Further examples from the nearby cultures of Sumer, Babylon and Assyria underline Niehaus's point: *the 'image' is the physical (human or statue) representation, and mediation of the presence, of a god.*

This may well be true in the wider ancient Near-Eastern world, but is there any evidence that we should understand *the Bible's* teaching about the image of God along these lines?[16] After all, just because a word is typically used by pagans to mean one thing, that doesn't necessarily mean that it must mean the same thing in the Bible. We must let Scripture interpret Scripture.

Niehaus concludes that we have in these ancient Near Eastern parallels 'adumbrations [foreshadows] of truth revealed in scripture'.[17] How so?

First, we can identify similarities between the description of the Egyptian king as the 'image of [an Egyptian] god' on the one hand, and the creation of Adam as a king over creation in the image of God on the other. As Victor Hamilton puts it in his commentary on *Genesis*, '[i]n God's eyes all of mankind is royal'.[18]

Second, Niehaus observes that in the ancient Near East, idols were typically placed in temples (or 'houses' – the word is the same in most of the relevant languages): 'The fact that a god's temple was his house implies a supernatural correspondence.' In other words, '[t]he temple and its furniture should correspond to their heavenly counterparts, just as the idol of the god corresponds to the god'.[19]

---

14 Ibid. 103. An 'archetype' is an original, or a pattern from which copies are derived.
15 Ibid. 105–106.
16 Michael Horton accepts the political roots of the biblical concept but rejects the religious roots as being hopelessly idolatrous. See Horton, *Pilgrim Theology*, 123. As I've suggested, it wasn't so easy to separate religion from politics in the ancient world. Both fields, I would argue, show us a debased version of the truth.
17 Niehaus, *Ancient Near Eastern Themes*, 110.
18 Victor P. Hamilton, *The Book of Genesis. Chapters 1–17* (Grand Rapids: Eerdmans, 1990), 135.
19 Niehaus, *Ancient Near Eastern Themes*, 91.

Does this make any sense of what we find in the Bible? It has been observed that in Genesis 1 (and arguably in the ancient Near East more generally) the entire cosmos is depicted as the temple of the Creator, and that this temple reflects the heavenly temple in which the Creator dwells.[20] Meredith Kline takes this one stage further, arguing that 'the garden of Eden was a microcosmic, earthly version of the cosmic temple and the site of a visible, local projection of the heavenly temple'.[21]

If we combine what we've learned about the typical meanings of the words 'image' and 'likeness' in their historical context, it seems at least possible that the Genesis account is describing man as the physical representation of God placed in God's cosmic temple (and microcosmically in the garden) to fulfil a position analogous to that of God himself in his heavenly temple.

Let's try and put these ideas in a diagram. Remember Van Til's diagram from chapter 1?

Figure 2.1 **God and creation**

The big circle represents God, and the small circle represents all of creation. The circles do not touch at any point. The diagram expresses the infinite qualitative distinction: *God is not like us.*

---

20 See e.g. G. K. Beale, *The Temple and the Church's Mission: A Biblical Theology of the Dwelling Place of God* (Leicester: Apollos, 2004).
21 Meredith G. Kline, *Kingdom Prologue: Genesis Foundations for a Covenantal Worldview* (Eugene, Ore.: Wipf & Stock, 2006), 49.

In fact, Van Til would always add two vertical lines to his diagram. The lines indicate that, because man is God's image, *even though God and man are infinitely different at every point,* man does in fact have a 'creaturely' *similarity* to God, standing as he does in a covenantal *relationship* with God. God has established this similarity and relationship. In other words, *God has made us like himself.*

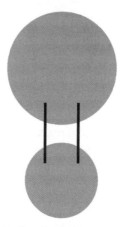

Figure 2.2 **God and creation in relationship**

But *in what way* are we like God? Well, think again about the idea of the 'image' of God. In pagan religions (which also employed this concept), a god is thought to live in a heavenly house or temple, often alongside other gods or goddesses. The 'image' of the god is a physical representation of the god, which mediates the god's presence/face to the worshipper. The image 'dwells' in an earthly house or temple, built of course by human beings, which is thought to be a copy of the heavenly house. We could express this idea in another diagram (see Figure 2.3 on p. 50).

The pagan 'god' is represented by the top circle with the letter 'g'. The top circle touches the bottom (earthly) circle, because gods and created things are thought to share the same being. (There is no infinite qualitative distinction in paganism.) The small house around the bottom circle is a man-made temple or shrine in which the image of the god (the smaller circle with the smaller 'g': biblically speaking, an 'idol') dwells. The earthly temple represents the heavenly dwelling

Figure 2.3 **The image of a god in pagan religions**

place of the god, just as the idol represents the god him- (or her-)self. In paganism people tend to think of the gods as being in some sense 'behind' their corresponding idols. This is illustrated by the touching or overlapping circles. The idol itself is not, strictly speaking, the god *itself*, but it may be treated *as if it were* the god because it represents and mediates or channels the god's presence. This is why the idol is considered worthy of worship. Now, of course inevitably this is a simplification. But I hope it helps you get the picture clear in your mind of what is going on when we find an 'image of [a] god' in typical pagan religion.

As Christians, needless to say, we know that we must 'flee' this sort of idolatry, and the entire mindset behind it (1 Cor. 10:14). We know that it is *false*: in Isaiah's words, '[w]ho fashions a god or casts an idol that is profitable for nothing?' (Isa. 44:10). Even so, there's something *attractive* about idolatry, to the sinful human heart at least. Instinctively, we want to *worship*. We instinctively ascribe ultimacy to something beyond ourselves, so much so that we human beings might well sing with Lumière in Disney's *Beauty and the Beast*, 'we only live to serve'. Eastern Orthodox theologian Alexander Schmemann has labelled humankind as first *Homo adorans* (man as worshipper) and only secondarily *Homo sapiens* (man as thinker).[22]

---

22 Alexander Schmemann, *For the Life of the World: Sacraments and Orthodoxy* (Crestwood, N.Y.: St Vladimir's Seminary Press, 2002), 14–15.

And this human instinct to worship – though warped – was not originally evil. We were made to glorify and enjoy the only true God for ever in worship of him alone. It is in our sinfulness that we've 'exchanged the truth about God for a lie and worshipped and served the creature rather than the Creator' (Rom. 1:25). Not all of those creaturely objects of our worship may be found in literal 'shrines' or 'temples'. This is why all Christians still need to heed the warning 'keep yourselves from idols' (1 John 5:21).

But here's the surprise: in *certain respects*, the biblical understanding of the relationship between the one true God and his 'image' (man) is similar to paganism, although there are also crucial differences. The next diagram represents the biblical view:

Figure 2.4 **The image of God in the Bible**

It looks a bit like the 'pagan' diagram, doesn't it? But there are differences. In the biblical view, God (the top circle with the capital G) dwells in his heavenly house/temple. The Bible tells us (in anthropomorphic language – I'll say more about language in the next couple of chapters) that God is seated on a throne (Ps. 11:4; Heb. 8:1; Rev. 4:2). His throne is in heaven – the uncreated heaven that is God's eternal dwelling place. But the book of Hebrews explains that there is an earthly 'copy and shadow of the heavenly things' (8:5). In context, the man-made 'tent' or 'tabernacle' (as described in the Old

Testament) is a copy of 'the true tent that the Lord set up, not man' (v. 2). As we've seen, the language of Genesis suggests that the garden of Eden is like a temple, and we've also noted Meredith Kline's argument that Eden is a microcosm (a miniature version) of the whole created universe.

I hope you can see that – if the world (and the garden of Eden, microcosmically) is rightly interpreted as a created 'copy' of the heavenly temple in which God dwells – it is to be expected that God would put his 'image' in his temple. And that is exactly what we find God doing in Genesis 1:26–27! Paganism 'knows' this principle. It simply distorts and twists it so that human beings end up worshipping created things instead of the Creator.[23]

In the biblical world view, man is the image of God (the small 'g' in the diagram above). What that means is that in the Bible, man is introduced as the concrete, physical representation of the eternal God. Man mediates and reveals the presence/face of God to the world. Just stop and think about that for a moment. This is a very high view of humanity, indeed. Every created man, woman, boy or girl *is* from the moment of creation or conception *the face of God to the world!*

Now, at this point we need to be as careful as ever to make clear the distinctions between truth and falsehood. In paganism, remember, the circles touch or overlap. Each pagan 'god' is thought to be in some way 'behind' its corresponding image. In interpreting the Bible, we must never forget our first theological key, *God is not like us.* The circles never touch. That is why we must never worship man (Acts 14:15) but God alone (Luke 4:8). For all that man mediates and reveals the presence of God to the world as God's 'image', *man is never God.* The true God is always 'above' and 'beyond' his image. He dwells in a high and holy place. But he has also placed his image in his cosmic 'temple' (the world) to reflect and show forth his glory. In other words, creation as the image of God ensures that there *is* a

---

23 What I am describing is, I think, an example of what theologian Dan Strange (following missiologist Hendrick Kraemer) calls the 'subversive fulfilment' of paganism by the gospel. See Strange's article 'For Their Rock Is Not As Our Rock: The Gospel As the "Subversive Fulfillment" of the Religious Other', in *Journal of the Evangelical Theological Society* 56.2 (2013), 379–395.

connection between God and man, established graciously by God in the beginning. It's precisely because of this God-given connection that man has his own (creaturely) versions of God's (divine) attributes, such as wisdom, power and love. These are, as we saw in the last chapter, infinitely distinct. But they are also, amazingly, *connected* – all these attributes in human beings are earthly copies of heavenly originals.

Biblical foundations 1: imaging the infinite

According to the Bible, man is the image of God. Remember our theological key for this chapter: *God has made us like himself.* What aspects of divine and human identity does this impress upon us?

First, let's think about God. In the last chapter, we've already considered the identity of God as the almighty Creator of the universe. Here we add to that picture: in creating human beings, God reveals himself as the one who desires and establishes *relationship*. The Bible is full of testimony to the ways that God *relates* to his human creatures. Just by way of a few examples, he speaks to them (Gen. 1:28), he sees them (Exod. 2:25), he knows them (Ps. 103:14) – knowing even the secrets of their hearts (Ps. 44:21) – he judges them (Ps. 9:8), he is merciful to them (Ps. 145:9) and he cares for them (1 Peter 5:7).

That God is profoundly relational towards us in this way is both *surprising* (because we are creatures of dust and he is an infinite, eternal spirit) but also *consistent* with his nature, as the one who is eternally love. We *are* creatures of dust, but we are not *merely* such: *God has made us like himself.* There is a sense in which, in creating man as his 'image', God loves himself. Again, this is an idea we must handle carefully. We should not imagine God narcissistically populating a world with multiple 'Mini-Me' clones for his own gratification. That would be a gross caricature, bringing God down to the human level in our thinking. It is entirely right that God should love himself, because he is pure goodness. As the pure, perfect, glorious Creator of all things, who is replete (full) in his own perfection, the will to create is a function of nothing but generous love. To be established as God's glorious image in his glorious temple, intended to reflect his glory to the world for ever is the highest privilege!

What, then, may we say of the Bible's teaching on man, created to be like God? Some precise theological terminology will help us as we think this through. We might sum up by saying that man is the *analogue* and *ectype* of God.

Analogue means 'a person or thing seen as comparable to another'. God is the incomparable one (chapter 1). And yet he has created something comparable to himself – man.

Ectype means 'a copy from an original: an imitation or reproduction'. It comes from a Greek word that means, literally, 'out of the mould'. In this case, the 'mould' is the *archetype* or *prototype*: God himself. My son looks a bit like me. As he gets older I notice him more and more starting to act like me too, just as my wife tells me I act like *my* father. When a son is like his dad, we might say he's *a chip off the old block*. It's surely significant that in the Bible, Adam, the first man, is called the 'son of God' (Luke 3:38). As God's 'son', Adam is also God's image and likeness. The biblical ideas of *image* and *son* are therefore related. Here are some implications of our being analogues and ectypes of God.

1. We're made to *reflect* God. This is, I think, the fundamental biblical concept behind the idea of the 'image' of God. Placed in God's earthly temple, the first couple and (by extension) their descendants were commissioned to *reflect* God, in a creaturely way, to the world. In other words, the face/presence of a human being was made to communicate, in an ectypal (copied) way, the face/presence of the invisible God himself. This means that *humanity reveals God*. We'll think more about how this relates to our knowledge of God when we come to the next pair of theological keys in this book.

2. We're made to *resemble* God. This doesn't mean that we can look in a mirror and see what God 'looks' like. God doesn't have a body. As we saw in the last chapter, God is spirit (John 4:24). What it *does* mean is that each of our attributes is, in some ectypal, analogical way, *like* God's attributes. God has made us that way, to resemble him. Do you love? It's because God loves (1 John 4:19), even because he *is* love (1 John 4:8). Do you laugh? It's because God laughs (Ps. 37:13), and not the other way round.

I'm going to make a bold claim: *everything* we do (except sin), we do because in some sense God does it first. At this point, some will begin to scoff, no doubt.[24] 'Come on!' they may say, 'I breathe, but surely you're not suggesting that God "breathes"?' Well, what about Genesis 2:7? Or 1 Timothy 3:16? (Both these verses speak of God's breathing.) Our instinct is probably to put the theological statement 'God "breathes"' in quotation marks, to show we're clear that God does not 'breathe' as we do, with lungs and air. But really, to be consistent, we ought to do this for every action God is said to do in the Bible: God 'laughs', and even God 'loves'. Why? Because *none* of these actions is the same as our human actions. Perhaps we even should say that God 'is', to show that his being is infinitely different from our being. On the other hand, if God's version of each action is the archetype (original) and our own is the ectype (copy) it might be better to put *our* actions in quotation marks: God loves, whereas we merely 'love'. I'm not seriously suggesting we really ought to adopt conventions like these: I just want us to see that we need to be biblically consistent in our thinking. We are made to *resemble* God, never (in any aspect of our being, knowing or doing) to *be* God. Again, more on this in later chapters.

3. We're made to *represent* God. This point is often acknowledged on the basis of the commission given to man in Genesis 1:28, 'Be fruitful and multiply and fill the earth and subdue it and have dominion over the fish of the sea and over the birds of the heavens and over every living thing that moves on the earth.' Sometimes

---

24 True, I don't want to make the patently ridiculous (not to mention blasphemous!) claim that God plays tennis, or digests food, or has sex, or a million other things you might think of that God clearly does not do. But what I am suggesting is that there is an analogy between each aspect of human life and God. E.g. God does not play tennis, but there is plenty of biblical evidence to suggest that he enjoys 'playing' in the sense of delighting in 'unnecessary' beauty. Think of a sunset or a waterfall or living creatures in their many colours. Our world is shot through with such beauty. God does not digest food, but he can certainly be 'satisfied' (Ezek. 24:13). Sexual union in marriage is an (ectypal) picture of Christ's relationship with the church (Eph. 5:32). Indeed, some from St Augustine to Peter Leithart have attempted – with, I think, varying degrees of success – to find specifically *trinitarian* patterns in created things, including human experience. See Peter Leithart, *Traces of the Trinity: Signs of God in Creation and Human Experience* (Grand Rapids: Brazos, 2015).

this idea is expressed in terms of *stewardship*: human beings are God's *stewards*. The word suggests careful, prudent management as God's servant. Others have suggested that humans are created as God's *ambassadors*. Again, the idea is of a particular kind of servant, this time one sent as an emissary of a sovereign. These are both helpful ideas. But I think that, given what we've seen in this chapter about the image of God, *regentship* is perhaps a more appropriate term. A 'regent' is a ruler who rules in place of the true monarch.[25] We've already noted the hints of 'kingship' in the Genesis account. It's true that man is given *rule* ('dominion' in the ESV) by God. As the image of God, man is set in God's place to have (God's) authority over the world. Of course, this authority is always derivative, and must not be abused. In this sense, the ideas of man as steward and ambassador are helpful, reminding us that the very highest calling for God's human creatures is always to serve Almighty God, whether as God's slave/servant (Deut. 34:5; Rom. 1:1), God's 'son' (Luke 3:38) or even as God's eternal Son in the flesh, a calling unique to Jesus Christ (Heb. 10:7).

One more aspect of man's 'representative' function is his special calling as a priest. Genesis does not say, in so many words, that Adam is a 'priest'. But the implication is strongly there, given not only the temple/tabernacle imagery of the garden, but also the specific language used. In Genesis 2:15, we're told that 'The LORD God took the man and put him in the garden of Eden to work it and keep it.' This specific double-responsibility ('work' and 'keep') is recorded in exactly the same words as the commission later given to the priests in the tabernacle/temple (Num. 3:7–8, translated as 'minister' and 'guard' in the ESV). As a priest, man is called to represent God to the rest of creation, and particularly to his fellow human beings, directing creation in the true worship of God.

4. We're made for *relationship* with God. We've already seen that God is the one who desires and establishes relationship with

---

25 Theologian John Murray says man is 'God's viceregent' (*sic.*). See John Murray, *Collected Writings*, 4 vols. (Edinburgh: Banner of Truth, 1977), 2:5. This is probably an error for 'vicegerent', as if man is only God's 'vice-' regent, it is unclear to me who Murray thinks God's *regent* is.

us. The other side of the coin is that we human beings are created for relationship, with God and with others. This relationship is based on true knowledge of God, which enables us to love (and serve or obey[26]) God with all our heart, soul, mind and strength, and to love others as ourselves (Matt. 22:37–39). Man is the only animal said specifically to be created male and female: once again, this underlines man's relationality, and even (in a qualified, human sense) human resemblance of God by means of the idea of the unity or coming together ('one flesh' in Gen. 2:24) of a diversity of persons.

Another question that has been much debated over the centuries is whether it is possible to 'lose' the image of God. Although some great theologians (like Martin Luther and even my great favourite John Owen!) have claimed that it is indeed possible, my biblical and theological instincts are to argue that the image cannot be lost. That is because the image of God – in the wider (essential) sense – is not something that man 'has': rather it is something that man *is*. To say that we are created as the image of God is like saying that we are created as God's offspring (Acts 17:28). While we live, we never cease to be what we are created to be. That's the way the Bible speaks of all people in the world. (See e.g. Gen. 9:6 and Jas 3:9.)

For the same reason, I don't think it's quite right to say that the image of God 'in us' has been 'damaged'. Biblically, the image of God isn't 'in' us. But I think we can, and should, recognize that *we **are** damaged images of God*. Holding on to the 'image' imagery, I have a picture of my children on my computer's home screen. The picture was taken with a (fairly old) camera on my phone, and so the resolution, or image quality, is not great. But it's still a good picture. If I were to adjust the resolution to make the image quality worse, the picture would become less and less of a good likeness. But it would still be an image of my children, even if it became so blurred that it was hard to identify them.

---

26 Love and obedience are never separated in the way that the Bible describes right human relationships with God. Obedience to all God's commands is closely tied to loving God in Deut. 6:1–9. Indeed, *love God* is itself a biblical command. As Jesus said, 'If you love me, you will keep my commandments' (John 14:15).

The biblical concept of the image of God is similar. Because of sin, we have become bad images. We don't *reflect* God as we should, and as a result we no longer *resemble* God, or *represent* God, or *relate* to God as we should. Even so, we are still images of God. As a human race, we are (collectively) God's image, but that image is damaged by sin. Individually, we are God's images, but those images are also damaged by sin. We'll think more about this in chapter 5, and in chapter 6 we'll consider how God is the one who restores the 'resolution' of his image by his Word and his Spirit.

Biblical foundations 2: Jesus Christ, the image of God

We could not finish this chapter without saying something about Jesus Christ. The Bible describes Jesus as the ultimate 'image of God'. John Calvin pointed out that this is true, not merely of Jesus' divinity, but also of his humanity.[27] In Colossians 1:15, Jesus is called 'the image of the invisible God, the firstborn of all creation'. 'Firstborn' here refers to Jesus' *pre-eminence*: he is given the highest honour above all things. It is a royal designation, fitting for the one who is called the ultimate 'Son' of God, 'the heir of all things, through whom also he created the world' (Heb. 1:2). In that same opening section of the letter to the Hebrews, the writer refers to Jesus as 'the radiance of the glory of God and the exact imprint of his nature' (v. 3).

Now, if I am correct about the meaning of man as the image of God, could we not say that *man* is, originally at least, 'the radiance of the glory of God and [God's] exact imprint'? I think the answer to this question is (a qualified) *yes*. Man was created to reflect the glory of God, and man is the 'exact imprint' of God.[28] Of course, as

---

27 See Horton, *Pilgrim Theology*, 336.

28 The Greek word is *charaktēr*, which means 'representation' or 'reproduction' (BDAG). Clement, Bishop of Rome, in his First Epistle to the Corinthians 33.4 (one of the earliest extant Christian texts apart from the New Testament, probably dating from the very late first century) suggests as much when he says in his account of creation that God 'formed man, the most excellent [of His creatures], and truly great through the understanding given him – the express likeness of His own image'. New Advent Translation, <http://www.newadvent.org/fathers/1010.htm>. Accessed 28 June 2019. The word *charaktēr*, translated

we've seen, this imprint is now faulty: the image is damaged. But there is a deeper-level difference between Jesus and Adam, even before Adam fell. The difference is this: only Jesus Christ is the exact imprint of God's *essence*, or *reality*.[29] That is because – uniquely – Jesus is *God* incarnate. As the apostle Paul put it, '[t]he first man [Adam] was from the earth, a man of dust; the second man [Jesus] is from heaven' (1 Cor. 15:47). The Person of Jesus Christ is an eternal, divine Person. He is no less than the Second Person of the Trinity, or God the Son. But this Person did also 'become flesh and dwelt among us' (John 1:14). He took to himself, for ever, human nature, in what theologians call a 'hypostatic union'. This means that his Person is now both human *and* divine. When we worship Jesus Christ, we don't worship his humanity per se – we worship the God-man, who brings us to the Father, in the Holy Spirit. All of this has massive significance for how fallen creatures (damaged images) can fellowship with God, an important subject to which we'll return.

Implications of the theological key

In this chapter, we've considered the theological key *God has made us like himself*. In this final section, it remains to unpack some of the implications of this key for our Bible-reading, doctrine and Christian living.

First, we must be careful to dismiss any view of God that denies he is *near* to us. Because God has made us like himself, there is a sense in which he has bound himself to us. This sort of binding relationship – of promise, reward and sanction – is called a

---

'express likeness' in this letter, is the same word translated 'exact imprint' in the ESV of Heb. 1:3. As should be clear, I don't think Clement quite gets the right biblical understanding of the image in his suggestion that man is the 'likeness of [God's] image'. (It's a good job that Clement's First Corinthians was not included in the New Testament canon – for my case at least! Clement's status as an 'Apostolic Father' means we may draw on his insights without committing ourselves to the ultimate authority of his teaching. His inclusion here is not, therefore, intended to 'prove' anything, but merely to illustrate my point.)

29 The Greek word translated 'nature' in Heb. 1:3 is *hypostasis*. BDAG defines this word as 'the essential or basic structure/nature of an entity, substantial nature, essence, actual being, reality'.

'covenant' in the Bible. The best theologies recognize that God established a covenant with man in creation.[30] According to this covenant, on the basis of our being created as his image, God *relates* to us. We must therefore reject the idea of **deism**. This is the philosophy that says God created the world, but since then he has had no direct involvement in or with it. Deism became popular during the Enlightenment, but it persists today in forms of agnosticism that acknowledge the likely existence of a higher 'power' but deny that power has anything to do with us.

On the contrary, biblically God is *near*. Of course, there is a sense in which God is near to his chosen people (Ps. 145:18). To believers, the Lord Jesus is 'at hand' (Phil. 4:5). But, as Paul preached at the Areopagus in pagan Athens, God 'is actually not far from each one of us' (Acts 17:27), including *all* human beings who image God. Quoting the philosopher Epimenides of Crete, Paul insisted that 'In [God] we live and move and have our being.' Even the third-century BC Greek poet Aratus had it right: 'we are indeed his offspring' (v. 28). The reason all humanity may be called God's 'offspring' is that man is created as God's image, bound to him in the closest of covenantal relationships.

As we read the Bible, we get a sense of this closeness. Right at the beginning, God was 'walking in the garden in the cool of the day' (Gen. 3:8). Although this account comes from after the fall, the implication seems to be that it was God's habit, hinting at close fellowship based on warmth, love and understanding. As I said in the last chapter, we must not think of God as inert or emotionless. He is, biblically, the Lover, the Husband, the Father, and so on. All of these pictures reveal God as (infinitely) passionate. Theologians speak of God's *immanence*. God is manifested in the world. He is not *merely* far off. He is with us. We'll see this immanence

---

30 See Hos. 6:7 (ESV) for explicit biblical mention of a covenant with Adam. I'm aware that there's some disagreement over the meaning of this verse, and although I think the ESV has translated it correctly, I'm not suggesting that the concept of the 'creation covenant' stands or falls on one verse of Scripture. The concept of 'covenant' is a rich, biblical, idea that expresses the way in which God relates to his creation, and the absence of the word 'covenant' in Genesis 1 – 3 does not mean that the biblical idea is not present (just as the absence of the word 'sin' in Genesis 3 does not mean the biblical idea is not present).

particularly as we consider Jesus Christ – *Immanuel* – 'God with us', but more of that later.[31]

In terms of our **worship**, the theological key *God has made us like himself* reminds us that *God fills his creation*. We'll think more about this in the next couple of chapters on the knowledge of God, but for now I just want to point out that worship of God is not an activity that's meant to transport us *out* of the (material, physical) world into some invisible and spiritual realm. God is in heaven, true, but he is also *here*. Sometimes people shut their eyes in order to 'worship'. I'm not saying that's wrong. But we ought to think about *why* we might do that. Yes – God is invisible. But God also fills creation. He has given us created things – bread, wine, water, words and *each other* – and appointed these as holy (set apart) means by which we must worship him. We shouldn't be embarrassed about these things. It's true that there's a dichotomy (and a choice to be made) between 'spirit' and 'flesh' in the Bible, but this distinction is *moral*, not one that's grounded in *being*. In terms of *being*, God has brought spirit and flesh together, above all in his image. There's nothing more intrinsically holy about our (human) spirits than our flesh. We mustn't cast these things asunder. We are called to glorify God with our bodies (1 Cor. 6:20) just as we are called to serve [worship] him with our spirits (Rom. 1:9).

Next, the theological key *God has made us like himself* must inform our **self-understanding and moral worth**. Although on one level we are creatures of dust – no more than clay pots crafted by the master potter – we are also 'God's offspring', created as his image. We must recognize that by virtue of our humanity we are created with a high, even royal, calling. Our thoughts, desires, words and actions have moral worth, and we are ultimately answerable to the judgement of our Creator for the way in which we have lived our lives. This principle of creation as the image of God must also affect our approach to human dignity, and therefore shape our response to such moral issues as abortion, euthanasia and all forms

---

31 'Immanence' and 'Immanuel' look like they might be related words, but in fact they are not. *'Immānû* is Hebrew for 'with us' and *'ēl* means 'God'. 'Immanence' is from the Latin *immanere*, meaning 'to dwell within'.

of abuse: physical, mental, spiritual and sexual. The male–female difference, and the *goodness* of that difference, is fundamental to the creation of man and woman as the image of God. This point should never be overlooked in discussion of questions of gender and sexuality.

In addition, the truth that *God has made us like himself* is important when we consider God's **salvation**. It is not surprising that God has a particular love for his image, for God loves himself. This is not to suggest that God was in some way obliged to save fallen man. The Bible makes it clear that salvation is all of God's grace. But it is, perhaps, the reason why fallen *man* is the object of God's salvation, but not fallen *angels*, who are not said to be created as the image of God.

Needless to say, this thought should be a spur to our **evangelism**. On the basis of the theological key *God has made us like himself* we should acknowledge that rejecting God is also rejecting oneself, at the level of one's very being. In calling people back to God, and to the true and ultimate image of God, who is God's unique Son and the Saviour, we are equally inviting them to recognize their own true selves. Once again, we see Calvin's point about how true knowledge of God and true knowledge of self are deeply inter-related. In addition, the fearful reality of hell is one that we must not try to tone down when we consider our motivation for sharing the gospel. For John Murray, it is precisely 'the fact that man is in the image of God that constitutes the unspeakable horror of eternal perdition [hell]'.[32]

Finally, the theological key *God has made us like himself* must have an impact on the way we **interpret Scripture**. As we saw in the last chapter, *God is not like us.* But in this chapter we've considered the other side of the dialectic: *we are like God.* Whenever we read about what God is like or what he does, we need to keep these two parts of the dialectic in mind, so that we can know God as he has revealed himself. As I've said, we don't try to fuse these two together into a hybrid of a God who is a bit like us and a bit unlike us. Instead,

---

32 See Murray, *Collected Writings*, 2:39.

we maintain both principles: the infinite qualitative distinction *and* the covenantal condescension by which God graciously binds himself for ever in love to his image.[33]

How might we summarize the first two chapters of this book? As Bruce Ware recognizes, our relationship with God can never be like any other relationship we have:

> Like it or not (and, by the way, by God's grace we should and shall like it if we do not now), this is not a relationship among equals, nor is it even a relationship with one older and wiser than myself. Rather, this relationship is radically unlike any human relationship, and one for which no explanation exists on the human level . . . The disparity between us and God is impossible really to imagine. Analogies fail, because the disparity here is between what is infinite and what is finite and, at present, fallen.[34]

We must not forget this relational asymmetry. Yet, at the same time, as Ware also correctly notes, amazingly 'the Father is *seeking* . . . people to worship him' (John 4:23; emphasis added).[35] This means that

> by God's grace and condescension, [relationship with God] is at the same time the epitome of what intimate and joyful relationship with another should be. And indeed, it is a relationship in which so much of the joy and fulfilment is found precisely in remembering always the infinite disparity that exists between God and us.[36]

---

33 In common speech, 'condescension' suggests an attitude of patronizing superiority. God's condescension is nothing like this. It is a function of his love: his making himself low for the sake of the lowly.

34 Bruce A. Ware, *God's Greater Glory: The Exalted God of Scripture and the Christian Faith* (Wheaton: Crossway, 2004), 156.

35 Ibid. 157–158.

36 Ibid. 159.

Questions for reflection or discussion

1 In what sense *are* you the image of God? In what sense are you *called to be* the image of God?
2 '*Everything* we do (except sin), we do because in some sense God does it first.' Do you agree? How might this affect the way you understand your vocation/calling in God's world?
3 How can the understanding of the image of God explored in this chapter help you in your evangelism?

3

We cannot comprehend God

God is incomprehensible. Even as I write these words, I can imagine some of my Christian friends' faces falling as they read. They are impatient with such things. 'Come on, Richard!' they say. 'We want people to *know God personally.* Doesn't the gospel say that's exactly what we *can* do? What's the point in telling people God is incomprehensible?' I'm sympathetic to these concerns. Like my friends, I want people to know God personally, and I thank God that is indeed possible by the gospel of Jesus Christ and the work of the Holy Spirit. But in this book, we're considering six theological keys to Scripture. And one of the things that Scripture lays down as fundamental about God is that *we cannot comprehend him.* In this chapter I'm going to explain and defend this key. And I hope that having done that, when we get to the next chapter (*God makes himself known to us*) we'll get a deeper and richer sense of the *gracious condescension* that underlies all human knowledge of God. In other words, the reality of knowing God personally will be one we experience all the more richly and thankfully as a result.

God: the great unknown?

God is incomprehensible. The word 'incomprehensible' is not used to describe God in the Bible, although it is found in various creedal or confessional statements of faith.[1] It does not mean that God is

---

1 See e.g. the *Westminster Confession of Faith*, 2.1. A common English translation of the Athanasian Creed (5th or 6th century AD), found in the Anglican Book of Common Prayer (1662), speaks of 'The Father incomprehensible, the Son incomprehensible, and the Holy Spirit incomprehensible.' In fact, the Latin word used is *immensus*. Philip Schaff, in his revision of the Book of Common Prayer translation, translates this as 'unlimited'. The ideas of immensity and incomprehensibility are closely related, as we'll see.

unknowable or completely unintelligible. Instead, it means that God cannot be *comprehended* – taken into the mind and mastered. On the basis of what we've already learned about the infinite qualitative distinction, this should be no surprise. Divine incomprehensibility means we cannot 'get our minds around' God. Or, in the simplest terms, we cannot know God fully, as he knows himself.

In this chapter, we'll consider, as before, the biblical foundations for the theological key, as well as its implications for our life and doctrine. In particular, we'll see that a robust commitment to divine incomprehensibility can help us when we get to the 'problem' passages of Scripture that describe occasions when God 'relents' or 'changes his mind'.

Biblical foundations

So, where in the Bible do we find this idea that God is incomprehensible? Actually, once you start to look for it, it's all over the place. Everything we've already seen of God's eternity, spirituality, immensity, impassibility, omnipotence and all the other divine attributes we considered in chapter 1 shouts divine incomprehensibility. For how can the finite (humans) contain or comprehend the infinite (God)? The Old Testament expresses this thought in various ways. For example, in Psalm 139 David says that God's knowledge (in context, God's omniscience in respect of human beings) is 'too wonderful . . . it is high; I cannot attain it'. In verses 17–18, David continues:

> How precious[2] to me are your thoughts, O God!
>   How vast is the sum of them!
> If I would count them, they are more than the sand.

The implication is that God's knowledge is far beyond human understanding. Psalm 145:3 says:

---

2 The *Hebrew and Aramaic Lexicon of the Old Testament* (*HALOT*) translates this word in Ps. 139:17 as 'difficult'. Compare the NET Bible translation 'How difficult it is for me to fathom your thoughts about me, O God!' See also Job's confession in Job 42:3.

> Great is the Lord, and greatly to be praised,
>> and his greatness is unsearchable.[3]

God's greatness cannot be 'investigated' by human wisdom: his depths cannot be plumbed. In the prophecy of Isaiah, God himself speaks to this effect:

> For my thoughts are not your thoughts,
>> neither are your ways my ways, declares the Lord.
> For as the heavens are higher than the earth,
>> so are my ways higher than your ways
>> and my thoughts than your thoughts.
> (Isa. 55:8–9)

In the New Testament, the apostle Paul concludes a long section of doctrinal exposition with the exclamation 'Oh, the depth of the riches and wisdom and knowledge of God! How unsearchable are his judgements and how inscrutable his ways!' (Rom. 11:33). For the apostle, the love of Christ 'surpasses knowledge' (Eph. 3:19). I want you to notice that this unknowability of God is not simply a consequence of sin and its distortions. It's true that sin affects our knowledge of God, and that is something we'll need to consider, but it's also true that *even without sin*, God would be incomprehensible to human beings.

God's thoughts are infinitely higher than our thoughts. God's knowledge of himself is therefore infinitely higher than our knowledge of him. What do we mean when we talk about 'God's knowledge of himself'? It should be no surprise to us that God *knows*. The Bible tells us that he is a 'God of knowledge' (1 Sam. 2:3). God knows all things. But perhaps you've not considered before the idea that God knows *himself*. Indeed, he must do so, for his knowledge is perfect and complete. God knows himself perfectly. Furthermore, on the basis of the simplicity of God (see chapter 1 above), God *is* his knowledge.

---

3   Literally, 'and concerning his greatness there is no searching'.

This is another of those ideas from systematic theology that, when I first heard it, seemed counter-intuitive to me. But bear with me for a moment. If God's knowledge were something separate from God's being, God would be divisible and he might – at least in theory – be God *without* his knowledge. The Bible will not allow us to conceive of God in that way. God's self-knowledge is expressed by Paul in 1 Corinthians 2:11, when he says that 'no one comprehends the thoughts of God except the Spirit of God'. God knows himself *by* himself. This is what we mean when we say that God has a theology. God knows himself, and indeed all things, by himself and through himself, completely and perfectly. This is God's 'theology'. Indeed, we may say that God's theology *is* himself. God is the Theologian, par excellence. He is the God (*theos*, in Greek) whose Word (*logos*) is comprehended by his Spirit. It is trinitarian. This divine (self-) knowledge is sometimes called *archetypal* theology.[4] We'll return to it in the next chapter.

We should recognize at this point, also, the intimate connection between God's *knowledge* and his *will*. Theologically (and biblically) speaking, these are not exactly the same thing. The Bible distinguishes them both verbally and conceptually. There are some things that God *knows* that he does not *will*. For example, we understand that God knows what is *not* going to happen tomorrow, yet he obviously does not *will* that to happen, otherwise it *would* happen! Those things that are not (but are nevertheless known to God) are called 'counterfactuals'. But, stated positively, we can say that if God *knows* something to be, we may take it that he *wills* it to be. In this sense, God's knowledge and will coinhere. That's why the Bible can sometimes assign God's sovereign appointment of all things to his knowledge (as in Acts 15:18), and sometimes to his will (or his 'plan' in the ESV of Acts 4:28, which is brought together with God's 'will' in Ephesians 1:11, where Paul writes of 'the counsel [the same word as 'plan' in Acts 4:28] of his will'.) John Owen puts it like this: 'As all things are present to [God] in one most simple and single act of his

---

4 I used the word 'archetype' in the previous chapter in our discussion of the 'image' of God to refer to an 'original' from which copies are made. It has a related meaning here, in our discussion of God's knowledge.

understanding, so with one individual act of his will he determines concerning all.'[5]

In contrast to God's knowledge, our (human) knowledge is by definition creaturely. As creaturely knowledge, it is exposed to the creaturely limitations of finitude. Our knowledge is also something that may be gained (and so increase) or lost (and so decrease). Some people are more 'knowledgeable' than others. As I get older, I find myself increasingly forgetful. Your knowledge and mine also rarely coincide with our wills. We do not have 'foreknowledge' as the Bible tells us that God has, and we have neither the power nor the singularity of purpose to carry out our wills in accordance with what we do know. That's why human plans are contrasted in the Bible with God's plans, as they are in Psalm 33:10–11:

The LORD brings the counsel of the nations to nothing;
    he frustrates the plans of the peoples.
The counsel of the LORD stands for ever,
    the plans of his heart to all generations.

The counsel and plans of the nations (human will, according to human knowledge) are frustrated by God. God himself, in contrast, is eternally unchangeable in his counsel and will. That is, of course, because God is unchangeable in his essence, and, as Owen says, if the purposes of God are eternal (which Scripture says they are), then 'they can be nothing but the very nature of God'.[6] In short, God is his purposes: his knowledge and his will.

As creatures, then, we are by nature limited in our knowledge. Some of the limitations of human knowledge may be consequences of the fall (see chapter 5 below) but others are simply factors of our being creatures, rather than the Creator. Pre-fall Adam had a close relationship with God, as we've seen. But even Adam didn't 'comprehend' God.

---

5 John Owen, *The Doctrine of the Saints' Perseverance Explained and Confirmed*, in *The Works of John Owen*, 16 vols. (Banner of Truth: Edinburgh, 1965), 11:142.

6 Ibid. 143.

Furthermore, there are some things that God simply chooses not to make known to us, even if we could understand them. For example, I don't imagine Adam fully understood all (or even most of) the consequences that would come from his eating the fruit of the tree of knowledge. I'm not trying to excuse Adam. Adam knew that he would die if he disobeyed (Gen. 2:17). I'm simply suggesting that Adam did not foreknow everything that would happen as a result of his sin. God did not let him have all of that knowledge. The gospel itself was, for many ages and generations, a 'mystery' (Col. 1:26). Likewise, God has not revealed most details about the future to us, even though God knows the future himself (Isa. 46:10). On one level, that is not because we *cannot* know these things. The knowledge of the day that I will die is not an *impossibility* for me to know, should God choose to reveal it to me. (Simeon was given knowledge a bit like this: see Luke 2:26.) On the other hand, my finitude and the fact that I am time-bound means it is entirely appropriate to my createdness that I should not know the future. There are surely many other things that God chooses not to make known to human beings (Deut. 29:29), presumably for our good.

The theological key *We cannot comprehend God* is the reason why Dutch theologian Herman Bavinck began his discussion of the doctrine of God with the famous words 'Mystery is the lifeblood of dogmatics.'[7] Bavinck goes on, '[T]he moment we dare to speak about God the question arises: How can we? We are human and he is the Lord our God. Between him and us there seems to be no such kinship or communion as would enable us to name him truthfully.'[8]

The distinctions between divine and human knowledge discussed above should help us when we come to those texts in the Bible that say God 'relents' or 'changes his mind'. Particularly, the truth that God does not know and will as we know and will can keep us from overreaching ourselves in what we think is going on in God's essence.

---

7   Herman Bavinck, *Reformed Dogmatics*, vol. 2: *God and Creation*, edited by John Bolt, translated by John Vriend (Grand Rapids: Baker Academic, 2004), 2.29. The two are not identical, but, for our purposes 'dogmatics' is Bavinck's word for what I call 'systematic theology'.

8   Ibid. 30.

A good example of such a text is found in Genesis 6. The scene is set before the flood, and we're told:

> The LORD saw that the wickedness of man was great in the earth, and that every intention of the thoughts of his heart was only evil continually. And the LORD was *sorry* that he had made man on the earth, and it grieved him to his heart.
> (vv. 5–6; emphasis added)

The Hebrew word 'regret' can mean to be sorry or to become remorseful (according to the *HALOT*). It is predicated of God frequently in the Old Testament.[9] But how are we to understand it? On the face of it, it seems as though God is surprised at how evil human beings have become. Somehow taken aback, God changes his mind, and follows a new, different course of action.

How are we to read texts like this one? Some principles based on our theological keys can help us.

First, we know now that we must not think of any act or state predicated of God in precisely human terms: *God is not like us.* There is always an infinite qualitative distinction to reckon with. God's regret is therefore as infinitely different from our 'regret' as God's knowledge is different from our 'knowledge'.

Second, we must take seriously other Bible verses that clearly state that God does *not* regret or change his mind. This point depends on the principle that *Scripture interprets Scripture*, so we can't interpret one part of the Bible in such a way that it contradicts another part. Rather, we're dealing with a dialectic. We've already noted in chapter 1 the denial that God changes his mind in Numbers 23:19, but we might add here 1 Samuel 15:29 ('the Glory of Israel will not lie or have regret, for he is not a man, that he should have regret'), along with Jeremiah 4:28 and Ezekiel 24:14 as example statements of God's *non*-regretting his own decisions and decrees.

---

9   See e.g. Judg. 2:18 (where it is translated 'sorry'); 1 Sam. 15:11; Jer. 15:6; 18:8; Joel 2:14; Amos 7:3. The 1 Sam. example is particularly interesting given the almost immediate caveat (using the same word in Hebrew for 'regret' or 'relent' in 1 Sam. 15:29). There are other examples of God's 'relenting' in the Old Testament: this is a representative selection.

Third, on the basis of the simplicity of God, we now know that each of God's attributes must be interpreted in terms of the others. This is explicit in Psalm 106:45:

> For their sake he remembered his covenant,
>> and relented according to the abundance of his
>>> steadfast love.

Here God's covenantal *ḥesed* (or his 'steadfast love', sometimes translated as his 'grace') is the context for interpreting his 'relenting'. The unchanging and unbreakable bond of love that God has freely established with his people becomes the backdrop for his apparent change of heart.

If we put these principles together, we can say that God certainly does 'regret' or 'relent' (for the Bible says that he does), but he does not do so in such a way as to compromise his other attributes. It is therefore best to understand God's 'relenting' or 'regretting' as referring to the way in which he is known by human beings, who (unlike God) *do* change.

Let me try to illustrate what I mean. I often bring a banana into my office for a snack, and, looking forward to eating the banana, at snack-time I open my bag. My attitude to the banana is 'positive', we might say. Once or twice I've forgotten about my banana and have left it in the bottom of my bag for a few days. By the time I find the banana again, it's gone brown and mushy, and I certainly don't want to eat it anymore. We could say that I now have a 'negative' attitude towards the banana. But here's the thing: the banana may have changed in the bottom of my bag, but I haven't changed. I still like ripe bananas. I still dislike overripe, mushy bananas. It's just that the (unfortunate) banana now experiences my negative rather than my positive attitude towards it, because *it has changed.*

Of course, like any illustration, this one has its weaknesses. Unlike God, I do change. I *might* actually come to dislike ripe bananas one day, or discover a fondness for mushy ones. God, on the other hand, does not change. Rather, he is 'experienced' as changing (his mind, or whatever) when changeable creatures present different aspects of themselves to him. Jeremiah 18:7–11 offers us a good example to think about. There God says:

> If at any time I declare concerning a nation or a kingdom, that I will pluck up and break down and destroy it, and if that nation, concerning which I have spoken, turns from its evil, I will relent of the disaster that I intended to do to it. And if at any time I declare concerning a nation or a kingdom that I will build and plant it, and if it does evil in my sight, not listening to my voice, then I will relent of the good that I had intended to do to it. Now, therefore, say to the men of Judah and the inhabitants of Jerusalem: 'Thus says the LORD, Behold, I am shaping disaster against you and devising a plan against you. Return, every one from his evil way, and amend your ways and your deeds.'

There are various 'if' conditional clauses in this passage. Notice that each time God lays down a condition for his 'relenting', it is a condition that depends on change in *some other agent* (in this case a nation or kingdom). We never find God saying in the Bible anything like, 'If I feel like it, I will relent.' It is true that God is utterly sovereign and free to do as he pleases. But he never breaks his own covenant promises, and he cannot deny himself (1 Tim. 2:13). Even in this particular passage it is clear that God is the one who 'shapes' and 'devises'. As we know from other places in Scripture, God is sovereign even over the leaders of nations and their hearts (Prov. 21:1). Their actions do not take him by surprise, even though they are, humanly speaking, free and responsible agents, who may (if the Lord so wills) be receptive to warnings and rebukes.

Theologian John Owen thus recognizes an aspect of God's will towards to his people that comprehends 'only external effects or products of the power of God'. In respect of this Owen says that God 'can pull down what he hath set up, and set up what he hath pulled down, *without the least shadow of turning*, these various dispensations working uniformly towards the accomplishment of his unchangeable purposes'.[10] Owen understands that God's purposes, to the extent that they are an expression of his will and therefore his very being, cannot change. It is God's creatures who change.[11]

Ultimately, then, we should conclude that God's regret and relenting are 'real' (these are indeed true things that we may say and know about God) but because they are *God's* regret and relenting, they are not like ours. They certainly do not mean that God is acted upon so that he changes in his being, or that God is caught off guard or thrown on to the back foot. Again, this is not to suggest that God cannot 'feel'. I have already suggested that in God's utter repleteness, he 'feels' maximally, always, for example, passionately loving goodness and righteousness and always passionately hating evil and sin. He is, therefore, genuinely grieved by human rebellion and idolatry, though this does not imply for one moment that his being is changed by such grief. Rather, such grief is the expression of his unchangeable being.

God's knowledge is his being. The two cannot be separated. But what can we say about *our* knowledge? How do we come to know anything? The Bible is not a textbook of psychology, physiology or neuroscience, but it does give us the bare bones of a human epistemology (theory of knowledge). In the next chapter, we'll think in more detail about what it means for human beings to know *God*, but here – in more general terms – we can compare and contrast human knowledge with divine knowledge. First, human knowledge, whether personal or propositional, is *gained* by *means* and *process* (Prov. 19:25; 21:11). Even the Lord Jesus in his human nature 'increased in wisdom and in stature' (Luke 2:52). Human knowledge is subject to frailty (Gen. 40:23) and error (Judg. 9:36). And this is before we consider the effect on human knowledge of sin, a subject to which we'll return in chapter 5.

---

10 Owen, *Doctrine of the Saints' Perseverance*, 134; emphasis added.
11 Bruce Ware speaks of God's 'relational mutability' alongside his ontological and ethical *im*mutability, and God's 'omnitemporality' alongside his eternity. See Bruce A. Ware, *God's Greater Glory: The Exalted God of Scripture and the Christian Faith* (Wheaton: Crossway, 2004), 143–146. I'm sympathetic to Ware's concern that we not deny God 'true' emotions, but I don't think Ware gives enough weight to the infinite qualitative distinction in his articulation of what it means for God to have 'emotions'; e.g. at ibid. 146.

Returning to our theological key *We cannot comprehend God* we may tighten up our definition at this point. If the Bible says that God 'relents', I think we can take it that he truly does so. The 'problem' (if that's the right word) is that we can never know what exactly this *means*. As many theologians have recognized, we can never know God's *essence* exhaustively. On one level, this is another way of saying we cannot know God as he knows himself. But it goes further: we cannot know God *as he is*. Once again, we must be very careful here. I'm not suggesting that the God we know is somehow not the true God, as though the 'real' God is always hidden to us, and that he might well be quite different from the God who makes himself known. If that were possible, God might be like the Wizard of Oz: putting on a mask that turns out to be a great cover-up. If that were so, we might be completely misled. As we'll see in the next chapter, the Bible assures us that God does, truly, make himself known to us. But we can never know his essence completely, even when we stand before him as glorified creatures, because before an incomprehensible God we'll always and for ever be just that: creatures.

Implications of the theological key

We need to stop and let the full force of this theological key sink in. It's impossible for us to know God as God knows himself. As the Swiss Reformer Zwingli famously wrote, 'What God is, we have just as little knowledge from ourselves as a beetle has of what man is.'[12] In fact – *from ourselves* – we have much less! We have to let this truth humble us as we approach Scripture, and as we approach God. We are fully known by God (1 Cor. 13:12) but our knowledge of him can only ever be creaturely knowledge, even when (as 1 Cor. 13:12 also says) the day comes when as glorified believers we 'shall know fully'. We must acknowledge the vast difference between our knowledge and God's. He is 'the only wise God' (Rom. 16:27), not because there are other 'unwise' gods to whom he may be compared, but because he alone is complete wisdom.

---

12 Ulrich Zwingli, *On True and False Religion*, ed. Samuel M. Jackson and Clarence N. Heller (Durham, N.C.: Labyrinth, 1981), 61.

Gregory of Nazianzus (329–90) suggested that there are three practical applications of our inability to know God's essence. First, it keeps us from pride; second, it increases our valuation of the knowledge of God that we do receive; third, it sustains us in our sufferings by directing us to the ever-deeper knowledge of God in the life to come as a reward for faithful service now.[13] In other words, divine incomprehensibility both humbles the believer and exalts God. As such, it's a powerful tool for our **discipleship**.

The incomprehensibility of God is one reason why 'face-to-face' encounters with God in the Bible are so overwhelming and humbling for the human beings who 'see' him. Of course, human sin is also an important factor here. For example, when the prophet Isaiah sees a vision of God in the temple, he hears the seraphim (angels) proclaim, 'Holy, holy, holy, is the LORD of hosts,' and cries out, 'Woe is me! For I am lost; for I am a man of unclean lips, and I dwell in the midst of a people of unclean lips; for my eyes have seen the King, the LORD of hosts' (Isa. 6:3, 5). It should not surprise us that human 'uncleanness' (sin) should cause fear – even despair – when facing the Holy One of Israel.

But in some other encounters with God in the Bible, the most overwhelming aspect of the vision seems to be the sheer *difference* (eternity, immensity, incomprehensibility, etc.) of God, compared to anything else in creation. Perhaps the best example of this is the prophet Ezekiel's vision. According to Ezekiel 1:1, the encounter begins when 'the heavens were opened, and [the prophet] saw visions of God'.[14] What Ezekiel actually saw is mysterious indeed: a vision of wind and fire (v. 4), 'living creatures' (v. 5) with wings (v. 6), and a 'wheel' (v. 15) with 'eyes' (v. 18). It was, to say the least, 'awe-inspiring' (v. 22). I take it that Ezekiel did not come to comprehend

---

13 Gregory of Nazianzus, *Orations*, 28.17–31. Scholars debate whether Gregory expected a definitive knowledge of the divine essence in heaven, or rather a fuller knowledge of God as befitting embodied creatures.

14 Despite appearances, this phrase need not in fact mean that the prophet had visions of God himself. The same Hebrew phrase is used in 40:2, when Ezekiel sees a vision that does not include a divine figure, but focuses on the rebuilt temple. It may mean visions *from* God, or (to use some technical grammatical terms) the genitive may be taken adjectivally: 'divine visions'. Does the prophet actually 'see' God in the vision in ch. 1? That is rather ambiguous, as we shall see.

God's essence in these visions, even though he was given voice to express one of the most mysterious theophanies (appearances of God) in the Bible. Yet what he did come to know was quite enough to cause him to fall on his face (v. 28).

I think there is an additional aspect to divine incomprehensibility that gives us much **consolation**, when we consider the difficulty we often have understanding the doctrines that the Bible teaches us about God, perhaps especially concerning his triunity. It is not surprising that we struggle here, because we are trying to understand an infinite God! Let us not be concerned about this. And let us not be ashamed to confess it to others. We are called, certainly, to love God with all of our minds (Luke 10:27), but we are not appointed to know him exhaustively, as if our finite minds could ever do that. As a friend of mine likes to say in his evangelistic conversations, 'The fact that we can't fully understand the God of the Bible is a strong indication that we're dealing with the true God.' I don't think that's just a cop-out he reverts to in order to dodge hard questions. God is, in every sense, above us, and transcends us in his knowledge just as he does in his being. As St Augustine said long ago, in a pithy maxim that I love, 'If you comprehend, it is not God.'[15] Beware the person who tells you they've got God worked out!

In Japanese (a language I speak) there is a helpful verbal distinction you can make between, on the one hand, merely doing something, and, on the other, doing something *completely* or *to the uttermost*. You just add the auxiliary verb *kiru* (to cut) on to the end of the main verb stem. For example, to *eat* in Japanese is *tabe-ru*, but to gobble up every last bite is *tabe-kiru*. To *be tired out* is *tsukare-ru*, while to be utterly exhausted is *tsukare-kiru*. Applied to knowledge, we may say of God's understanding that he *wakari-kiru* (he 'understands

---

15 This soundbite is actually a paraphrase. The whole passage of Augustine's sermon says, 'What then, brethren, shall we say of God? For if you have been able to comprehend what you would say, it is not God; if you have been able to comprehend it, you have comprehended something else instead of God. If you have been able to comprehend Him as you think, by so thinking you have deceived yourself. This then is not God, if you have comprehended it; but if it be God, you have not comprehended it. How therefore would you speak of that which you cannot comprehend?' Augustine, *Sermon 2 on the New Testament*, 52.16, New Advent translation, <http://www.newadvent.org/fathers/160302.htm>. Accessed 5 July 2019.

completely'). On the other hand, it's biblically axiomatic that no human being can ever *wakari-kiru* God.[16] Even to suggest this would be biblically blasphemous! Our knowledge of God is always partial and to some extent provisional.[17] We must say that even Jesus Christ according to his human nature did not fully comprehend God.[18]

The Reformer Martin Luther famously made a distinction between God as 'revealed' and God as 'hidden'. For Luther, God as he is in his infinite majesty is hidden to us. Luther was, in part at least, reacting to the medieval approach to the doctrine of God, which he thought tended to claim too much knowledge of God's essence. This problem has resurfaced at different times in history and in the work of different theologians, who, in the words of Donald Macleod, have 'given the impression that they knew what God has for breakfast'.[19] In a different context the apostle Paul warned the Corinthians 'not to go beyond what is written' in Scripture (1 Cor. 4:6). This is a warning we ought to take to heart as we read and speak about God. As we'll see in the next chapter, although we do not (and cannot) have complete knowledge of God's *essence*, we know him truly through his *energies*, as he condescends to reveal himself to us. The attributes of God that we learn from the Bible are always partial – but at the same time *accurate* – descriptions of God's ineffable (unspeakable) essence.

Just as our ontological limitations are actually gifts from God we may joyfully accept, so also are our **epistemological limitations**. It is *good for us* that we do not know many things. We've already considered how that might be so concerning the future. We can see, perhaps, how knowing the time of our death may not be helpful information for us to have. But we can also take it on trust that it is

---

16 There's a similar distinction in New Testament Greek between the verbs *ginōskō* (to know) and *epiginōskō* (to know exactly, completely, through and through), although based on biblical usage the distinction in meaning is not always clear-cut.

17 I say 'to some extent' without suggesting that our knowledge of God now gives way to something *entirely* different later, notwithstanding 1 Cor. 13:8–9.

18 In Jesus' case, knowledge of God was available not just from revelation (in the world and in Scripture), but was communicated from his divine nature in what theologians call the 'hypostatic union'. Even so, if Christ's human nature was fully and truly human (which it was) we must insist that he did not comprehend God according to his human nature.

19 Donald Macleod, *Behold Your God* (Fearn: Christian Focus, 1995), 9.

good for us not to know why many things happen, either to us personally, or in the wider world. Sometimes (like Job) we might dearly like to know why troubles come, but this is not the best thing for us, or God would surely have given us that knowledge (Rom. 8:32). Also, we can rest in the truth that God's knowledge of us as individuals is perfect. As our Creator, God fully knows us (Ps. 139:1–5; 1 Cor. 13:12). This is, in Scripture, a reason for us to be comforted, just as it was for the Israelites before the exodus (Exod. 2:25) and for future generations who heard the story of God's mighty redemption.

This chapter is the shortest in this book, only two-thirds the length of the other chapters. Perhaps that is appropriate because of all the theological keys this is the one that should most reduce us to silence. In encountering the God of the Bible, we are confronted with the absolute and the infinite. We, on the other hand, are contingent and finite creatures, dependent on him for our every breath, for the perceptions of our senses, for the rules of logic and for the firing of each brain cell. *We cannot comprehend God.*

> Be not rash with your mouth, nor let your heart be hasty to utter a word before God, for God is in heaven and you are on earth. Therefore let your words be few.
> (Eccl. 5:2)

Questions for reflection or discussion

1 How could you explain to a non-Christian God's incomprehensibility? Why would you want to?
2 What does it mean when Scripture says that God 'regrets'?
3 What are the potential gains for Christians who recognize God's incomprehensibility?

4

God makes himself known to us

'To the unknown god'

This was the unusual inscription on an altar that the apostle Paul found in the city of Athens during his second evangelistic journey of AD 49–52 (Acts 17:23). In Paul's day, Athens was still the cultural and intellectual centre of the known world. It was a city filled with idols and what Paul referred to as the many 'objects of your worship', but this altar stood out for Paul because the object of the Athenians' worship was apparently unknown even to them.

The Greek word for 'unknown' in the inscription is *agnōstos*, which of course gives us the English word 'agnostic'. But the Athenians seem to have been different from most modern-day agnostics. Today, agnostics typically cite the unknowability of God or gods as grounds for *not* worshipping (at least as far as they understand worship). In contrast, this Athenian altar appears to have been designed precisely for the worship of the 'unknown' god by the 'very religious' Athenians (v. 22). Does this altar suggest that at least some of the people of Athens were aware of the existence of a divine being greater than all their idols, one who 'does not live in temples made by man' (v. 24)? Whatever the intention of the altar-builders, Paul seizes on the evangelistic opportunity: 'What therefore you worship as unknown [the (different) word this time means 'that about which you are ignorant or unaware'], this I proclaim to you' (v. 23)! The true God, Paul says, is *knowable*. Indeed, he *must* be known. As Paul explained, there had been 'times of ignorance' in the past (v. 30), but such ignorance has been wilful and culpable disobedience, in respect of which God will punish the unrepentant by his appointed judge, Jesus (v. 31).

As we saw from the theological key of the previous chapter – *We cannot comprehend God* – knowing God is never something to be taken for granted. The finite (my mind, or yours) can never contain the infinite (God). And yet, the Bible teaches clearly that knowledge of God is both possible and pervasive: in a certain, general sense, *everyone* knows God. Over 300 years ago, Swiss theologian Francis Turretin argued that there are no 'atheists properly so called'.[1] Turretin's point was that created man knows deep down that there is an infinite God, possessing eternal power, who gives man his being and identity. This is a biblical idea.[2] In denying this God, the purported atheist cuts off the source of his own life. In the twentieth century, Cornelius Van Til expressed a similar idea: 'A little child may slap his father in the face, but it can do so only because the father holds it on his knee.'[3] For Van Til, the 'atheist' is the little child, and God is the father. Even the act of rejecting God is an act that is possible only because God gives the life and breath to do it. Just so, according to the apostle Paul, certain things about God are 'clearly perceived' by all (Rom. 1:20).

But this does not mean that all people now know God in the same way. In another, special sense, God gives saving knowledge of himself to his covenant people who are the particular object of his love. This knowledge of the only true God and of his Son Jesus Christ, given by the Holy Spirit, is what Jesus refers to as 'eternal life' (John 17:3).

Saving knowledge of God is of course made necessary by sin. In chapters 5 and 6, still to come, we'll be thinking about the theological keys to Scripture that relate particularly to *acting*, and it's there that we'll turn our attention to what the Bible says about God's saving acts (including his giving of the gift of saving knowledge), and the human ethical responses that these acts of God call forth. In this chapter, I don't intend entirely to 'bracket out' the problem of sin.

---

1 Francis Turretin, *Institutes of Elenctic Theology*, edited by James T. Dennison Jr, translated by George Musgrave Geiger, 3 vols. (Grand Rapids: Baker, 1992), 1:177.
2 See Rom. 1:18–21.
3 Cornelius Van Til, *The Case for Calvinism* (Phillipsburg: P&R, 1979), 147.

As a sinner myself, how could I do that? For a start, most of what the Bible tells us about God's making himself known to creatures concerns *sinful* creatures.

There's a category of sin that theologians call *noetic* sin.[4] It relates particularly to the mind or to knowing, and this cannot be side-stepped. True, Christians are those who have their minds renewed (Rom. 12:2), but we Christians continue to struggle with sin, including in our thinking and knowledge. This is probably the main reason why true Christians disagree about doctrine or about what the Bible teaches. We are, I suspect, far too quick to suggest that the Bible is 'not clear' about a certain point when the lack of intellectual clarity is more likely to be our own. So, as I argued in the previous chapter, all our knowledge is subject to both human limitations and human sin. This applies particularly to our knowledge of God.

Even so, in this chapter, I want to keep us to a limited focus. We're still thinking primarily about epistemology here, that is, we're focusing on the Bible's characters as 'knowers'. I want us to think biblically and theologically about how God 'makes himself known' to finite human beings, so that we can understand more deeply how we relate to God. Remember, knowing God is still a theological 'problem' even without the complicating factors of human sin and God's judgement of sinners. If we don't recognize the problem, that's perhaps a sign we haven't yet really got to grips with the theological key from chapter 3, *We cannot comprehend God*, and perhaps also the theological key from back in chapter 1, *God is not like us*.

Despite the 'problem', the Bible insists that God is knowable. How so? Chapter 2 (*God has made us like himself*) has already given us some hints as to how God makes himself known to creatures. We saw there that God made human beings as his image, partly in order to reflect his glory to the world. One aspect of reflecting God's glory is making him known. Human beings make God known (partially, of course) to one another. When God makes something known

---

4 From Greek *nous* (mind).

to creatures, theologians call this **revelation**. The God of the Bible is a *revealing* God. Let's now turn to the Bible and see how the theological key *God makes himself known to us* is grounded there, and what the Bible means when it tells us that God makes himself known.

Biblical foundations

I probably don't need to convince any readers of this book that God is a revealing God. But I want us to go back to the Bible to investigate – and try to summarize – what it says about *how* God reveals and *what* God reveals. This should help us to get to the bottom of what it means to say, biblically, that human beings can know God. We'll begin our investigation in the Old Testament.

Old Testament

There is no word for 'revelation' as a noun in the Old Testament. Instead, there are three key Hebrew verbs for us to consider. The three verbs in their reflexive forms literally mean 'show oneself', 'make oneself to be seen', and 'make oneself to be known'. When God is the subject of any of these verbs, we are getting close to the biblical concept of revelation.

God 'shows' or 'shows himself'[5]

When God is the subject of this verb, it has a special, theological sense. God may be said to show either *himself* (as in Gen. 35:7, the first example of this use in the Bible) or *something else*, such as the announcement or disclosure of information.

Other examples of self-showing (such as 1 Sam. 3:7, 21) indicate that *knowing* the Lord is closely related to the Lord's *revealing* himself. These verses suggest that God's self-revelation to Samuel was typically in the form of *the word of the Lord*. Indeed, there's not always a clear distinction to be made between God's revealing *himself* and his revealing a *verbal message*. In Isaiah 22:14, the Lord

---

5   This is the Hebrew verb *niglāh*, or *gālāh* in the qal (active) form.

reveals *himself* to the prophet 'in [his] ears', with specific verbal content following.[6]

Another well-known example of this verb is Deuteronomy 29:29, a verse we've looked at more than once in this book. God isn't the explicit subject, but it's clear that he is the one doing the revealing: 'The secret things belong to the LORD our God, but the things that are revealed belong to us and to our children for ever, that we may do all the words of this law.' This verse is significant because of the distinction it makes between the 'revealed things' (in this case, from the context, *tôrâ*, or God's law/teaching) and the 'secret things'. It suggests that whatever God chooses to reveal to human beings is not *exhaustive*, but *sufficient*. That of course fits with what we saw in the previous chapter: God is incomprehensible, which just means that he cannot be known exhaustively, rather than that he cannot be known at all.

More significant uses of this verb in a revelatory sense are found in the book of Isaiah. In Isaiah 23:1, God's 'oracle' or pronouncement (presumably in the form of communicated information) is revealed. In 40:5, the prophet announces a time when the 'glory of the LORD' will be revealed, and all flesh shall *see* it together. In 53:1, the 'arm of the LORD' is revealed, in poetic parallel with a 'report' to be believed. In 56:1, God's righteousness is revealed.

The only other use of this verb in the Old Testament that is obviously connected with divine revelation is in Daniel 10:1. In that verse, a 'word' is revealed to Daniel. We're not told whose word it is, but it is a 'true' word and the implication is that it is from God. Interestingly, the word revealed to Daniel is connected with a 'vision': this same word is translated 'appearance' in verse 6. Not

---

6 Compare the biblical uses of the Hebrew idiom 'uncover the ear', usually translated 'revealed' in the ESV. E.g. in 1 Sam. 9:15, we read that the Lord had 'revealed to Samuel' (literally, 'uncovered the ear of Samuel') *so that* the Lord might speak a specific word to him. That specific 'word' is the actual, verbal content of v. 16. There's a similar use of this idiom in 2 Sam. 7:27, where the Lord reveals to his servant David his plans to build David a house. Again, certain specific content is said to be revealed by God. The same idiom is in the parallel to 2 Sam. 7:27 in 1 Chr. 17:25. It is also found, again with God as the subject, three times in the book of Job (33:16; 36:10, 15).

for the first time, hearing and seeing are closely related in God's revelation.[7]

To sum up, this word, which means 'show oneself', is perhaps the most important Hebrew word connected with revelation in the Bible but we've now discussed almost every appearance it makes in the Old Testament with this meaning. You may have been surprised how infrequently it's used. What do the other two verbs – 'make oneself to be seen' and 'make oneself to be known'[8] – add to this picture?

God 'makes himself to be seen'

God 'shows himself' to (or 'makes himself to be seen' by) the patriarchs Abraham, Isaac and Jacob in the book of Genesis (12:7; 17:1; 18:1; 22:14; 26:2, 24; 35:9; 43:8). The ESV translates all of these verbs as 'appeared'. Similarly, God 'appeared' to Moses in the book of Exodus (3:16), to Manoah in Judges 13:21–22, and to Solomon in 1 Kings 3:5; 9:2–9. God also 'appeared' to the whole people of Israel at the tent of meeting in Leviticus 9:4. In 1 Samuel 3:21 (a verse we've already noted above) God's 'appearance' (literally his 'causing [Samuel] to see' himself) is closely related to God's self-revelation. It is helpful to see that the causative meaning 'showed himself' or 'caused himself to be seen' is behind the English translation of these verbs as 'appeared'. This is clearly a *visible* manifestation of God: he *makes himself* to be *seen*.

We may well wonder *what exactly* it was that was seen, given that it is axiomatic in the Old Testament (and, for that matter, the New Testament) that God *cannot* be seen. We'll come back to this important question in a moment, when we consider the precise relationship between 'revelation' and God.

---

7 In Dan. 2 (which is mostly written in Aramaic rather than Hebrew) the equivalent verb in Aramaic appears seven times. Perhaps most interesting is v. 46, in which King Nebuchadnezzar describes *both* God as a 'revealer of mysteries' *and* God's servant Daniel as one who is (by divine revelation) 'able to reveal this mystery' to the king. In this case, God reveals himself *through* Daniel.

8 In Hebrew, *nir'āh* and *nôdā'* in the niphal (passive or reflexive) forms.

God 'makes himself to be known'

This verb is first found with God as its subject in Exodus 6:3b. In that verse, it's negative ('I did *not* make myself known' to the patriarchs by the name the LORD) but the sense is that the LORD *did*, positively, make himself known (by his name the LORD) to Moses. Ezekiel 20:5 (and also v. 9) looks back to the events of the exodus as the time when the Lord particularly 'made [himself] known' to his people Israel. Future promises that God will again 'make himself [myself] known' come later in the book (35:11; 38:23). The second of these verses is interesting because God promises to make himself known 'in the eyes of many nations'. The revelation is beyond Israel, and is expressed in a visual idiom (in the 'eyes'). There are some further uses of this verb in respect of God in the Psalms (9:16; 48:3). In the poetry of Isaiah 66:14, both 'the hand of the LORD' and his 'indignation' (the expressions are in parallel and probably refer to the same thing) will be 'made known'.[9]

One more important verse to consider here is Jeremiah 31:34, part of the prophecy of the new covenant. In this verse, the LORD promises a day when *all* people ('from the least of them to the greatest') will *know* him (the basic, active [qal] form of the verb). This knowledge is clearly caused by God himself: the LORD is the one who (in v. 33) 'will put [his] law within them, and . . . write it on their hearts'.

Drawing the above data together, it's possible to make some general comments about revelation in the Old Testament on the basis of the biblical uses of these verbs when God is the subject:

First, **what God reveals** can be either

1 God himself or
2 a specific attribute of God, such as his righteousness, or glory, or power (I take reference to God's *arm* to be a metonym for his strength, rather than a literal description or even a simple anthropomorphism[10]) or

---

9 Again, there is an equivalent verb in Aramaic, found in Dan. 2:23, 28–30, 45.
10 A metonym is a word used as a substitute for something else with which it is closely associated, such as saying 'Downing Street', when we mean the Prime Minister or his office. Anthropomorphism means, in this sense, attributing human characteristics or behaviour to God.

3 God's 'word', understood in either general terms (as in
   e.g. 1 Sam. 3:7, where God's word is the subject of the passive
   verb), or specific terms, as a particular, defined utterance.

Second, **the recipients of God's revelation** can be either

1 individual human beings or
2 a large group of human beings (such as all God's people) or
3 'all flesh' (which refers either to all human beings, or possibly
   even to all created animals, birds and fish as well).

In particular, God seems to cause himself to be *seen* and/or *known*
at *times of special significance in salvation history* (e.g. to the patriarchs, at the exodus, in some future revelation to the nations, and in
the new covenant, etc.).
   Third, **God's revelation has two aspects**, or modes. It is

1 auditory (hearing), and
2 ocular (seeing).

When God reveals, that revelation is therefore either (or both) *verbal*
and/or *visual*.[11] What, then, of the New Testament?

New Testament

The most important New Testament term for 'revelation' is *apokalypsis*, so we'll focus our attention on it here. It's the name commonly
given to the last book of the Bible, based on the first word (in Greek)
of Revelation 1:1. From that single verse, we can already make some
interesting observations. Revelation is 'given' by God, it's 'of' Jesus
Christ (which could mean either that it's 'about' him or 'from' him,
or possibly even both), and it's given with God's purpose or intention
of 'showing' (a word that speaks of making something apprehensible

---

11 There's a nice example in the first two chapters of the book of Isaiah of how these two
aspects (the verbal and the visual) can come together. In 1:1 we read about '[t]he *vision* of
Isaiah the son of Amoz, which he saw concerning Judah and Jerusalem', while 2:1 begins,
'The *word* that Isaiah the son of Amoz saw concerning Judah and Jerusalem' (emphases
added). Both 'vision' and 'word' are 'seen' by the prophet.

to the senses, without specifying *which* sense) to his servants 'what must happen very soon'. It seems reasonable to conclude that the entire book is the (verbal) content of the revelation, although there is visual content given to John also.

Apokalypsis (and its verbal form, *apokalyptō*) is found in various other places in the New Testament. There are three main uses of this word group that are relevant for the present study.

First, 'revelation' relates to God's making *things* known. Such 'things' include divine instruction of various sorts, and above all what theologian John Gill (1697–1771) called 'the instruction of the gospel'.[12]

These revelations might come to the prophets of the Old Testament. For example, in 1 Peter 1:12 that which was made known to the Old Testament prophets is said to have been 'revealed' to them.

The apostles of the New Testament are also recipients of revelation. For example, the apostle Paul received the gospel itself 'through a revelation of Jesus Christ' (Gal. 1:12). Again, this might mean that the revelation Paul received was 'about' Jesus Christ or 'from' him, or possibly both senses are intended. For Paul, the gospel was something that had once been a 'mystery' (in the sense that it was previously unknown or veiled) but the mystery was now made manifest in his own time: this uncovering is described as a 'revelation' in Ephesians 3:3–5.

Sometimes, the revelations that Paul and others in the churches received seem to have been more specific to their own circumstances. Such revelations might have involved divine guidance in respect of decisions to be made, as is apparently the case in Galatians 2:2. Something similar happens in Acts 11:28 when the prophet Agabus 'foretells' (a rare verb that is also used with Jesus as the subject in John 12:33; 18:32; 21:19) a coming famine. Paul links 'revelations of the Lord' to special 'visions' that he had received in 2 Corinthians 12:1, 7. At other times, revelation was given to the wider church through the charismatic gifting of individual church members.

---

12 John Gill, *Exposition of the Bible*, Prov. 23:23, <https://www.biblestudytools.com/commentaries/gills-exposition-of-the-bible/proverbs-23-23.html>. Accessed 15 August 2019.

For example, in 1 Corinthians 14:6 'revelation' is connected with 'knowledge', 'prophecy' and 'teaching' in the context of spiritual gifts. There is a similar use in verse 26, connected with public worship.

It's not entirely clear how these sorts of 'revelations' relate to the revelations of the prophetic word of God in the Old Testament, and the gospel. I don't want to get sidetracked here into a debate about charismatic gifts because that's not the main point of this book. But I think it's legitimate to conclude that – whatever we think these charismatic 'revelations' were or are – they are not as important as the revelation that is given through the prophets and apostles to the entire church of Jesus Christ for all time. The prophetic word given to Agabus about the famine was certainly useful for those who originally heard it, and for the brothers in Judea who received a financial gift as a result. But in itself it's not much use to you or me.

In the ministry of Jesus himself, there's a very important passage about revelation in Matthew 11:25–30 (with a partial parallel in Luke 10:21–22). It's worth looking at it in detail.

> [25]At that time Jesus declared, 'I thank you, Father, Lord of heaven and earth, that you have hidden these things from the wise and understanding and revealed [*apokalyptō*] them to little children; [26]yes, Father, for such was your gracious will. [27]All things have been handed over to me by my Father, and no one knows the Son except the Father, and no one knows the Father except the Son and anyone to whom the Son chooses to reveal [*apokalyptō*] him. [28]Come to me, all who labour and are heavy laden, and I will give you rest. [29]Take my yoke upon you, and learn from me, for I am gentle and lowly in heart, and you will find rest for your souls. [30]For my yoke is easy, and my burden is light.'

'These things' (in v. 25) may refer, in the immediate context in Matthew, to the coming judgement of the unrepentant cities of Israel. But given that the context for a very similar saying in Luke is quite different, it seems reasonable to allow 'these things' a wider reference, perhaps even to *all of Jesus teaching ministry*. If that is correct, then Jesus is saying that his teaching has been 'revealed' to some (the 'little children', probably a reference to those who humbly depend upon God) but 'hidden' from others (the 'wise and understanding', most likely referring to those who are 'wise' in their own eyes). Note that this – even the 'hiding' part – is said to be a **good** thing! Jesus *praises* his father for it. It is a function of God's *'gracious will'* (literally, his 'good pleasure'). There is something *discriminatory* about this kind of revelation.

Second, 'revelation' relates to God's making *himself* known. In verse 27 (still in Matt. 11), Jesus says that he himself ('the Son') is the one who, originally, *knows* the Father, and also the one who, in turn, makes his Father known by 'revealing' him to others. This revelation is *personal*. It is not so much a revelation of divine instruction, as it is a revelation of God *himself*. The recipients of this revelation are distinguished as Jesus' *choice*. Even so, in verses 28–30 Jesus offers a general invitation to *all* who 'labour and are heavy laden' to come to him for rest. As elsewhere in Scripture, divine sovereignty in election is taught alongside a universal gospel call.

In Galatians 1:16, Paul says that God was 'pleased to reveal his Son to [literally, 'in'] me. Once more there is a stated divine purpose behind this revelation, namely that Paul should 'preach [Christ] among the Gentiles'.

Revelation is thus, in these texts, the work of both the Father and the Son. At the same time, the *object* of revelation may also be said to be either the Father or the Son. On the one hand, as in Matthew, the *Son* is said to reveal the *Father*. On the other hand, as in Galatians, *God* (the Father) is said to reveal the *Son*. As the eternal Word of God (John 1:1) the Son of God became flesh in order to dwell among us (John 1:14) so that finite human beings might hear, see and even touch 'the word of life' (1 John 1:1).

What about the Holy Spirit? As we might expect, he too is involved in revelation. In Ephesians 1:17, revelation is presented as a trinitarian work of God, but it is a work particularly appropriated to the Holy Spirit. Here the Spirit's revelation is closely associated with divine 'wisdom' and the 'knowledge of [God]' – in this case, the intended sense is *knowing* God, rather than knowledge *about* God. Likewise, the Spirit is the agent of revelation of the 'depths of God' in 1 Corinthians 2:9–13.

Finally, there is a notable use of *apokalypsis* in Luke 2:32 (part of Simeon's song – the so-called Nunc Dimittis), where Jesus Christ himself is identified as both God's 'salvation' (v. 30) and a 'light for revelation'. The Lord Jesus himself is revelation light, given by God to a dark world.

Third, 'revelation' relates to the disclosures of the 'last days'. In many ways, this third category is a composite of the first two. God is said to reveal things that are yet future, just as the future is itself characterized personally as the revealing of God himself. But it is better to keep these references separate from the first two types, because they concern things that have *not yet* been revealed, and they therefore constitute a separate idea in Scripture – that of an ultimate *revelation to come.*

In 1 Peter 1:7, the apostle Peter speaks of 'the revelation of Jesus Christ'. It is clear from the context that Peter is talking about a future, personal appearing of Jesus at the time of his second coming in judgement. Later in the same letter (4:13), Peter speaks of Christ's *glory* being revealed in the future. Paul uses similar terms as Peter in 1 Corinthians 1:7 and 2 Thessalonians 1:7. In Romans 8:18–19 there is a remarkable reference to 'the glory that is to be revealed to us', and to all creation's 'eager longing for the revealing of the sons of God'. This 'revelation' is best understood as God's making known the true destiny of his children in the new creation.

In summary, this brief study of *apokalypsis* in the New Testament yields similar findings to our previous examination of the Old Testament. 'Revelation' may be understood either (or both) *propositionally* and/or *personally.* In revelation, God uncovers that which has hitherto been unknown, hidden or mysterious. In the New Testament, revelation is usually given to individuals, but the revelation received is to be (for the most part) passed on to others. Above all, revelation is centred on the saving work of God. While the offer (or gospel call) is extended to 'all', the recipients of revelation – in the sense of those who acknowledge and accept it – are, by the grace of

God, those 'chosen' by Christ, or elected by God to receive saving knowledge.

The *apokalypsis* word-family is not the only set of terms used in the New Testament that are related to revelation. A full study would require us to give attention to the use of words for declaring, imparting, expounding, showing and making known. But for the most part, *apokalypsis* 'tends to absorb the synonyms and provides the context in which we are to understand their theological use'.[13] One important exception, which in many respects stands alone and requires further discussion is the key term 'word'. This is not the place to give a full account of the 'word' of God in the Bible, but we may at least consider it in relation to some verses in the letter to the Hebrews. The first three verses of the letter read like this:

> [1]Long ago, at many times and in many ways, God spoke to our fathers by the prophets, [2]but in these last days he has spoken to us by his Son, whom he appointed the heir of all things, through whom also he created the world. [3]He is the radiance of the glory of God and the exact imprint of his nature, and he upholds the universe by the word of his power. After making purification for sins, he sat down at the right hand of the Majesty on high . . .

These verses helpfully summarize a number of the themes we've already seen from our brief survey of both Testaments of the Bible:

1 **God has spoken.** As I've suggested above, the Bible shows us that God's *speech* is one of the main forms of revelation. As the writer to the Hebrews makes clear, God's speech came in 'many ways': we should expect to find great variety in it.
2 **God spoke to his people in the Old Testament by the prophets.** The writer to the Hebrews is talking about the Old Testament prophets.

---

13 G. W. Bromiley, 'Reveal; Revelation', ed. Geoffrey W. Bromiley, *The International Standard Bible Encyclopedia, Revised* (Grand Rapids: Eerdmans, 1979–1988), 161.

3 **God has spoken to his people in the New Testament by his Son, through the apostles.** 'Us' in verse 2 probably means 'all us Christians'. But in 2:3 the writer spells out the process by which this happened: the message or 'word' (*logos*) of salvation 'was declared at first by the Lord, and it was attested to us by those who heard'. Taken together, these verses show that God spoke a message (*logos*) 'by' his Son (Jesus) to the apostles ('those who heard'). That message was then attested as the authoritative, apostolic message from God, and so the writer (who has received and now faithfully passes on the *logos*) can say that God has spoken to all Christians 'by his Son'.

4 **The Son reveals God because he is in the closest possible relation to God.** The Son, it seems, doesn't just speak a message *about* God. He is called the 'Word' of God (John 1:1) but also 'the radiance of the glory of God and the exact imprint of his nature' (Heb. 1:3). As such the Son truly and ultimately *reveals God*. That's why Jesus may say, 'Whoever has seen me has seen the Father' (John 14:9). Again we see here how *hearing* and *seeing* come together in God's revelation. The Son of God is not just *eloquent* (speaking) but also *effulgent* (shining).

So, the God of Scripture *makes himself known*. That's our theological key for this chapter, and I hope I've demonstrated that it's the teaching of the Bible, from start to finish. God is a revealing God, and central to what God reveals is *God himself*. As theologian Millard Erickson says, revelation is 'God's manifestation of himself' or 'God's communication of himself'.[14]

But there's another important question we need to consider here. When God reveals himself, what does he reveal? We might further unpack the question like this: 'If God is incomprehensible in his essence, what is the exact relationship between God and his revelation? Are they the same thing? Or different? And why does that matter?'

---

14 Millard Erickson, *Christian Theology*, 2nd edn (Grand Rapids: Baker, 1998), 178.

Is God the same 'thing' as God's revelation? In this chapter, we're going to try to work out an answer that is both faithful to Scripture and theologically coherent.

Why does this matter? Well, on a very basic level, if God = God's revelation, then the Bible cannot be revelation (in any simple sense) unless we want to say that the Bible = God, and I take it no readers of this book would want to affirm that! On the other hand, if God ≠ God's revelation,[15] we may still have a problem if we want to insist that God somehow reveals *himself.*

Perhaps the best way to approach this question is to think first of a human 'revelation'. You probably don't know me personally. Because you're reading a book that I've written, you do know some things about me. You know that I'm a Christian and that I write about theology, for example. I have revealed those bits of information to you. In order for you to know me better, you need more revelation. But what about knowing me *personally*? For that personal knowledge, 'information' about me is insufficient. I have to reveal *myself.* I might do that as you see me face to face, and as we talk, or as you watch how I act in certain situations.

Is such revelation *me*? On this human level, the answer has to be 'no'. Biblically, as we've seen, 'I' am a psychosomatic (body and soul) union and so even when you receive my personal revelation you don't receive *me*. Again, we can compare this with the doctrine of God's simplicity. God's knowledge and his essence coincide completely. My knowledge and yours, however, is not the same as our being. Even in marriage, which is the closest human relationship, I and my wife remain separate.

How does this apply to God?

We've seen above, from the Bible, that God reveals or has revealed either (1) himself, or (2) something about himself (which could be [i] an attribute of himself,[16] or [ii] information about himself), or (3) something else. We've also seen that he does this either (a) visually,

---

15 The symbol ≠ means 'does not equal'.

16 As we've already seen in this book, according to the traditional Christian understanding of God, an aspect or attribute of God *is* God. In other words, (2)(i) in the above paragraph is, properly, the same as (1). This is the consequence of God's being 'simple'. God's 'simplicity' means that – unlike us – he is not made up of different parts.

and/or (b) verbally. The divine agent of revelation can be either (A) Father, (B) Son, or (C) Holy Spirit – indeed, often all three Persons are involved.

Now, we need to do some theological 'heavy-lifting'!

When God reveals *himself*, **to himself**, he is not only both subject and object of the revelation; he is also the indirect object of the revelation. What sort of revelation are we talking about here? This is what is described in Matthew 11:27, where Jesus talks about how the Father makes himself known to the Son. We can safely assume that such revelation is complete. God makes God known to God. 1 Corinthians 2:10 seems to describe something similar, when it says that the Spirit (of God) 'searches . . . the depths of God'. As I say, this revelation is complete, without remainder.[17] Clearly, in this case God = God's revelation.

When God reveals himself **to human persons**, his revelation is certainly true (by definition, given his character as true) but it is not complete. That is not so much because God chooses to hide certain aspects of himself from human beings,[18] as it is because God is infinite and we are finite. Theologians use technical terms to make this point. God's knowledge of himself, they say, is **archetypal**. Our knowledge of God, based on what God has revealed, is **ectypal**.[19] God's self-knowledge is the **archetype**. Our knowledge is the **ectype**, or copy, of God's knowledge.

---

17 What does it mean for God to reveal himself to himself? There is a good deal of mystery here. As human beings, we cannot do this, even in an analogous sense. We are not triune. We can, for sure, learn new things about ourselves, but God does not do that. His self-knowledge does not come about incrementally, or through a process of discovery. He reveals himself (and therefore knows himself) from and to all eternity. Some may wonder how Matt. 24:36 ('But concerning that day and hour no one knows, not even the angels of heaven, nor the Son, but the Father only') fits in. The most satisfying understanding of this is that the Son of God limited his knowledge in certain respects in his incarnation, including in respect of the time of his return.

18 Of course, there are the 'secret things' of Deut. 29:29, which we considered in chapter 1. Also, we can acknowledge that God does not reveal himself to the human race 'all at once', as it were, but rather 'progressively' over time. However, I incline to the view that the 'secret things' are not so much aspects of God's character that he does not make known (such as e.g. a divine attribute that he has never told us about, if such a thing were conceivable), but rather aspects of his knowledge (of his essence or his will) that are not revealed to us because either (1) we couldn't understand, given our limitations as finite creatures, or (2) it would not be good for us to know, for some reason of God's own.

19 These terms were introduced in chapter 2 above.

So, let's return to our main question: Is God the same 'thing' as God's revelation? The answer, *when what God reveals to us is* **himself**, is *yes*. But what happens is not precisely the same as what happens when God reveals himself to himself, because we cannot know God as God knows himself. All we can know is a copy, or ectype, of God's knowledge of himself.[20] The question is: Is this copy also God?

The answer to that is a bit complicated! Ectypal knowledge of God (or the 'copy' of God's being that is revealed to us) is known first to God before it's known to us. God 'forms' the copy, in his own mind, perfectly and in such a way that we can receive it. This copy is still God, but it's now God, not in the form of his essence, but in accommodated form, before such revelation has ever been received by any human person. Once a human being actually *receives* ectypal knowledge of God (or God's self-revelation), that God-made copy faces distortion, corruption and error. Until we get to heaven, we will never have 'in ourselves' perfect revelation, or knowledge of God. Nevertheless, by the work of the Holy Spirit we can trust that whatever errors or corruptions do enter our theology, they will not be such that true knowledge of God is impossible.[21]

We have seen already that we don't (ever) get to know God's essence comprehensively. Such knowledge is impossible for finite, created beings. Rather, we come to know God through his outer works of creating, preserving, redeeming and judging the world. In these works, God freely re-presents himself to us in 'accommodated' form that is appropriate to our understanding. He speaks to us, as Calvin suggested, in baby-talk, as he 'lisps with us as nurses are wont to do with little children'.[22] As God does this we can truly come to know him by way of his 'energies', which are pointers (accurate but partial) to his essence.[23]

---

20 Remember that, on the basis of God's simplicity, God's knowledge = God.

21 In this section, I'm heavily dependent on the classic treatment of the knowledge of God in Franciscus Junius, *A Treatise on True Theology*, translated by David C. Noe (Grand Rapids: Reformation Heritage, 2014).

22 John Calvin, *Institutes of the Christian Religion*, edited by John T. McNeill (Louisville: Westminster John Knox, 1960), I.13.i.

23 On the essence–energies distinction, which has its roots in Eastern theology but is appropriated by John Calvin, among others, see Michael Horton, *The Christian Faith: A Systematic Theology for Pilgrims on the Way* (Grand Rapids: Zondervan, 2001), 129–130.

Now, a final question: Where is true knowledge of God to be found? The surprising answer that the Bible gives us is that knowledge of God is to be found in *created things*. That's surprising – or it *should be* surprising, I think – because of the infinite qualitative distinction. As we saw in chapter 1, in his *being* (essentially) God is not like anything in creation. That's why we cannot comprehend his essence (chapter 3). But, God has made copies of himself. We've seen that in chapter 2, where I suggested that human beings are analogues, or ectypes of the divine archetype. Above all, Jesus Christ is the image of God, in whom all God's fullness dwells (Col. 1:15).

But more than this, we may say that *everything in creation* reveals the knowledge of God. That was Paul's argument in Romans 1. It's what the psalmist means in Psalm 19 when he says:

The heavens declare the glory of God,
  and the sky above proclaims his handiwork.
Day to day pours out speech,
  and night to night reveals knowledge.
(vv. 1–2)

The (visible) heavens declare God's glory, and so does the visible earth. Created things image God. It's true that only the Lord Jesus Christ is the perfect image of God, but other things – not just human beings – reflect God in partial, but just as true, ways. Garry Williams explains:

A rock, for example, images the dependability of God, but it does not image the fact that he is alive. A lion images his strength, but it does not image his wisdom. Fire images the way he consumes sin, but it does not image that he does so rationally and in a controlled way. Created things are both like God [as we saw in chapter 2 of this book] and different from him [the subject of chapter 1]. In the ways they reflect his perfections they are like him, but in their finitude they are unlike him.[24]

---

24 Garry J. Williams, *His Love Endures for Ever: Reflections on the Love of God* (Nottingham: Inter-Varsity Press, 2015), 37.

God reveals himself in the things that he has made. So, all of creation is revelation. Theologians call this 'general' revelation. It's given to all. In contrast to this, 'special' revelation is given only to some. This special revelation is historical. God *acted in history*, in mighty acts of salvation, which we'll consider in chapter 6. It's also the revelation of which the Bible itself is a stream. God spoke in the past. And it's right for us to think of the Bible as God's revelation (rather than merely a 'witness' to revelation) because God can and does speak to us still in the creaturely words of Scripture, to give us ectypal knowledge of what he is like, so that we can know him, love him and worship him. When God speaks today, making himself known, his Holy Spirit is still active, taking the words of Scripture and illuminating them in the hearts of his chosen people so that they believe in the gospel. We can 'think God's thoughts after him'[25] because of the covenantal connections that God has established between his own mind, the minds of his human images and the world in which we live.

Implications of the theological key

All human beings really do know God, however suppressed or distorted that knowledge may be. And we really can know him savingly, if he graciously reveals himself to us. God wills to make himself known to his people, so that they may enjoy him for ever. What are the practical applications of the theological key *God makes himself known*? We may begin with our approach to the Bible. As we read Scripture, we should expect to know God personally, and more deeply, as he reveals himself to us. That is not an automatic outcome of Bible-reading, as though we could write the equation *human mind + Bible = knowledge of God*. Scripture tells us about the necessary continuing work of the Holy Spirit, and the human approach to reading or listening that is appropriate to the Bible's character as the written Word of God. Also, when God does reveal himself in and through Scripture that will happen in different ways, no doubt, as

---

25 This expression is attributed to the scientist Johannes Kepler (1571–1630).

we read different types of literature in the Bible. God does not reveal himself in Exodus in the same way he does in Proverbs. But it is the same God who makes himself known throughout the Bible. The God of the New Testament is the same as the God of the Old Testament. Jesus Christ is always the same: yesterday, today and for ever (Heb. 13:8). The sense of difference is just that we encounter his words at different points in the history of special revelation and at different points in our own lives. Again, our knowledge of God will always be incomplete, and that is true even if we were somehow to understand and know all of the Bible at once, for God infinitely transcends his revelation to us.

We ought also to look for the true knowledge of God in the created world around us. General revelation cannot save us because we cannot know about Jesus the Saviour and the work of the Holy Spirit without special revelation. But wearing the 'lenses' of special revelation, as it were, we can be renewed in our minds to find true knowledge of the world and of other creatures that points us back and up to God, helping us in our understanding of the many 'earthy' images that the Bible uses to communicate God to us.

In our Christian lives, we should expect knowledge of God to be *useful* for us. God reveals himself for a purpose, which in the lives of his people is a *saving* purpose, namely to conform them to the likeness of his son, and to dwell with them eternally in a renewed creation (Rom. 8:29; Jer. 32:38; Rev. 21:5). John Owen received this sort of knowledge, and he longed for others to share in it: 'Whatsoever of his name he holds out to the sons of men, it will be a strong tower and place of refuge and safety to them that fly unto it.'[26]

Knowing God is of course a good thing. It's right for us to want to know God better, and to pray this for others, that they might know him (for the first time) and know him better as they grow in faith, hope and love, which cannot be separated from the true knowledge of God. That's Paul's prayer in Ephesians 3. He prays that the Christians in Ephesus

---

26 John Owen, *The Doctrine of the Saints' Perseverance Explained and Confirmed*, in *The Works of John Owen*, 16 vols (Banner of Truth: Edinburgh, 1965), 11:132.

may have strength to comprehend with all the saints what is the breadth and length and height and depth, and to know the love of Christ that surpasses knowledge, that you may be filled with all the fullness of God.
(vv. 18–19)

This is a great prayer for us to pray for others, and for ourselves. Notice that for Paul, the love of Christ 'surpasses knowledge'. 'Surpassing' in the original Greek comes from the verb *hyperballō*, which has the literal sense of 'throwing over' and was originally used in spear-throwing contests when one athlete outperformed the others [BDAG]. In terms of our knowledge, Christ's love is *hyperballistic* – exceeding all other human understanding. Nevertheless, it's precisely *this* love that Paul wants the Ephesians to 'know' and 'have strength to comprehend'.[27] This is not some special 'gnostic' knowledge available only to a select few. It is for 'all the saints'. And the fruit of such knowledge is that men and women 'in Christ' may be 'filled with all the fullness of God', including knowledge (3:19). What amazing blessings we have in the gospel in and through our Lord Jesus! No wonder Paul can bless the God 'who has blessed us in Christ with every spiritual blessing' (1:3).

Even though knowing God is the greatest blessing – so much so that Jesus can equate it with eternal life – the Bible contains warnings for us that there is a type of knowledge that is dangerous for us. This is knowledge without love (1 Cor. 13:2), the sort of 'knowledge' that 'puffs up' rather than 'builds up' (1 Cor. 8:1). In 1 Corinthians, we discover that the true knowledge of God comes from and through the Holy Spirit, who reveals this knowledge to God's people. Paul explains how this works. First, God decreed a 'secret and hidden wisdom of God . . . before the ages' (2:7). Next, Paul tells us that the Spirit himself is the only one who 'comprehends the thoughts of

---

27 A similar dialectic is found in Eph. 3:8, where Paul says that he preaches 'the unsearchable riches of Christ'. By the preaching of the Gospel and the work of the Holy Spirit, the unsearchable is searched, and the incomprehensible comes to be known. Paul revels in this sort of idea. In Rom. 11:33–35 he uses the same word 'unsearchable' when describing the 'wisdom and knowledge of God'. 'Inscrutable' though God's ways may be, the Spirit has made them known in the gospel – sufficiently for the salvation of all who believe.

God' (2:11). Then, believers receive the same Spirit 'that we might understand the things freely given us by God' (2:12). The Spirit – God himself – is our Teacher (2:13). True knowledge of God comes only through him. Amazingly, Paul concludes that the 'spiritual' person (the one who has received the Holy Spirit, or the Christian) has 'the mind of Christ' (2:16). If you are a Christian, you share, by the Spirit who fills you, in a measure of God's own knowledge!

This astonishing epistemological dialectic (*We cannot comprehend God / God makes himself known to us*) tells us what happens at the gospel's bedrock. Michael Horton puts it like this:

> In his revelation, the God who cannot be possessed makes himself our richest treasure; the one who cannot be mastered makes himself the servant of our redemption; the one who is high and exalted makes himself lowly and the greatest sufferer of human injustice and hatred who ever lived. Yet, wonder of all wonders, even in loving us in this way, God remains transcendent, incomprehensible, and hidden.[28]

I should stress that in laying out the systematic theological keys in these terms, I'm not saying we need to 'reformulate' the gospel, or tell the story differently. Horton's quote above is brilliantly put, but it still needs to be supplemented by the biblical story of *Creation – Fall – Redemption – Restoration* or some similar account of what God has done, is doing and will do. However, as I've done throughout this book, I want to show you the relationship between the biblical 'characters'. Let the understanding that you can truly know the incomprehensible God because of his condescension and love towards you cause you to lift your heart and voice in praise, and to commit yourself again to loving and serving him for the rest of your days! God has indeed acted to save his elect, and now calls you to respond. We'll think more about these actions and responses in the final two chapters of this book, beginning with the 'bad news', before we get to the 'good news'.

---

28 Horton, *Christian Faith*, 129.

Thou incomprehensible but prayer-hearing God,
Known, but beyond knowledge,
revealed, but unrevealed,
    my wants and welfare draw me to thee,
    for thou hast never said, 'Seek ye me in vain'.[29]

Questions for reflection or discussion

1 In what sense does every human being know God?
2 How, why, what and to whom does God reveal?
3 How can we know God better? Are there any potential
  dangers to be avoided as we gain this knowledge?

---

29 Arthur Bennett (ed.), *The Valley of Vision: A Collection of Puritan Prayers and Devotions* (Edinburgh: Banner of Truth, 1975), 11.

5

Our sin separates us from God

'What do you do?' It's one of the first questions we often ask when we're getting to know someone. When I worked as a pastor in Oxford I once met a scientist who told me she spent her time researching what makes particular hens attractive to cockerels.[1] That gave rise to a second question: '*How* do you do that?' . . . which very quickly became a third: '*Why* (on earth) do you do that?'. These questions certainly led to an interesting conversation! The same questions are also helpful to ask when we're thinking about the Bible's main characters – God and human beings.

Importantly, the Bible's special insight into these questions tells us that both God and human beings do certain things based ultimately on what kind of persons they are. I may be able to choose my job (whether researching sexy chickens or whatever), but *ethically* my choices are defined by who I am, just as God's 'choices' are defined by who he is.[2] More than that, the ethical value of the things we do (including the things we think and say) define our relationships, with one another and with God.

Acting it out

Back in chapters 1 and 2 we began by asking 'Who (or *what*) is God?' and 'Who (or *what*) is man?'. It's worth reminding ourselves of our main conclusions so far. Biblically speaking, God is the transcendent one, utterly filled with all of his own fullness from all eternity and in need of nothing outside himself. Indeed, in eternity past there *was* nothing outside God. At the same time, God is revealed in the Bible

---

1 Or, in the USA, roosters.
2 This is not to deny our freedom, within certain limits, to make choices.

to be the Creator of all things, out of nothing.[3] In his being – and in all of his attributes – God is infinitely distinct from everything else that now is. But his relationship to his creation is not merely one of transcendence. God is also immanent: present in and to his creation. Indeed, God has created all things to show forth his glory, by *revealing* himself to the world through what he has created. Supremely, God has created man (human beings) as his *image*. We are royal heirs and regents who reflect, resemble and represent God himself to one another and to the world. Human beings are made for relationship – with one another and with God. At the heart of this relationship for which we are created is the privilege of *knowing* God personally, by his Son and his Spirit. We've seen that this knowledge is never comprehensive, but it is enabled by God, who establishes a correspondence between his own (archetypal) self-knowledge and the (ectypal) knowledge of creatures. Human beings can – and *do* – know God.

The theological keys that we've been considering in this book are therefore deeply *personal* and *relational*. They are not mere intellectual puzzles, somehow disconnected from real life. God *is*. We (human beings) *are* because God *is*, and God has made us 'like' himself. Our life is in him. God knows all things. And he communicates a measure of that knowledge to his creatures, including the knowledge of himself. 'We love because he first loved us' (1 John 4:19), just as we *know* because he first *knew* us, and *are* because he first *is*.

Up to this point, we've focused our attention on the categories of *being* and *knowing*. In these final two chapters, we move on to think in particular about *acting*. In this chapter (chapter 5), we'll consider what it means for God and human agents to 'act', what the Bible says about who we humans are *ethically* and what this means for our relationship with the God whom the Bible calls the 'Holy One'. In the next chapter (chapter 6) we'll see that the most important acts of God after creation relate to the salvation of the world through the personal love-gifts of his Son and his Spirit. Finally, we'll think about

---

3 Just to be clear, 'nothing' is not a thing, or substance, out of which God created, despite what some theologians say. It is just that: *no thing*.

the human acts that are called forth as a response to this work of God's love.

As we do this, we're going to focus our attention more directly on two 'characters' in the Bible story. I said back in the introduction to this book that the main 'characters' in Scripture are God and man. That's true. But in these final two chapters, our focus will be on two individual men: Adam (this chapter, in particular) and Jesus (the next chapter, in particular). There's good reason for this: Adam and Jesus have a unique significance for theology. These two men are related to us in different ways, and those relations reveal to us what kind of relationships have been established between God and man. What Adam and Jesus do (or did), as well as *how* they did it and *why* they did it, affects you and me.

Adam is, of course, the 'first man' (1 Cor. 15:45). We saw back in chapter 2 the significance of Adam's creation as God's image. But when the Bible calls Adam the 'first man', more is meant than a simple acknowledgement of the fact that Adam is the physical father of the human race, who came along before anyone else. To use the terms I have introduced in this book, calling Adam the 'first man' is as much a *theo*-logical statement as a *chrono*-logical one. Adam has a profound and continuing significance for us, which we'll explore in a moment. Similarly, Scripture calls Jesus Christ the 'second man' (1 Cor. 15:47). This is obviously *not* a mere chronological designation. It's true, of course, that Jesus came *after* Adam (notwithstanding the 'bombshell' statement of Jesus in John 8:58 about Abraham – here Jesus is referring to his eternal existence with God, along the lines of John 1:1). But there were many, many generations between Adam and Jesus. Jesus is singled out as the 'second man' in the Bible for his *theological* significance. In addition, as we saw earlier on, Jesus is the *God*-man. He has both a divine and a human nature. As the eternal Word of God, Jesus Christ *is* theology. He is theology personified. But theology does not stop with Jesus Christ. Jesus does the works of his Father (John 10:37) and makes the Father known (John 1:18). As the only way to the Father (John 14:6) Jesus makes possible the true knowledge of the God who sent him into the world. Such knowledge is eternal life (John 17:3).

By way of preliminaries, we need to establish a few basic points about what it means to 'act', both for God and for human beings. It may seem obvious that both God and humans do *act*. The Bible speaks of God's 'mighty acts' (Deut. 3:24; Ps. 145:4). As far as human beings go, we've even got a book in the New Testament called the *Acts* of the Apostles. But as you might expect me to say by now, divine acts and human acts are infinitely different.

Let's start with human beings, because we are a bit easier to understand than God is. When you or I act, we do so as the outcome of our *will*. We will to do something, and that's why we do it. If I eat a banana (my act), it's because I will to act in that way. In the simplest terms, we always do what we will (or *want*) to do. Now of course it is possible – theoretically at least – that I might be forced to eat a banana against my will. But in that case, most people would recognize that it's not really *me* who has acted. It's not my act if it's forced upon me. In such circumstances, I'm passive or manipulated.

Why do I will to do certain things? The answer to that, biblically, is that my 'heart' (Bible-language for the moral 'control centre' of my life) is inclined to will in certain ways. Our intentions arise from the thoughts of our hearts (Gen. 6:5). Our hearts may overflow with both good and evil (Luke 6:45, see also Ps. 45:1), and what comes out of us (out of our mouths, specifically, in the case of Jesus' teaching in Luke 6) reveals the state of our hearts.[4] This is the biblical grounding for the truth that we act *freely*, in the sense that we always do and say what our hearts desire. That in turn grounds our moral *responsibility*, for we are accountable for our actions: they really are *our* actions. More on this in chapter 6. Of course, as creatures we are subject to change, and that includes change of our hearts and wills. That means we might will to do something one day (and do it) but then no longer will to do it the next day (and so stop). We are not always able to act according to our wills.[5] Even when we *are* so able,

---

4 Not everything we do necessarily or obviously has moral value one way or another. Whether I eat a banana or not need not reflect the 'goodness' or 'evil' in my heart.

5 I don't mean this here in a *moral* sense (although that sort of inability is important and we'll come back to it) but in a *physical* or *natural* sense. E.g. I may will to open a door but it turns out to be locked, or I may will to marry a certain person but that person refuses me, and so on. Most of these examples of inability can be attributed to my lack of either

our wills are influenced by a whole range of outside factors and information (some of which may well be 'fake news') and we usually come to a fixed decision of the will by means of a process of deliberation. We are also unable to know all the consequences of our actions.

What about God? Some theologians tells us that God is 'pure act'. If you're encountering this idea for the first time, it may sound quite bizarre to you. What does it mean? Traditionally, it underlines the point I've already made a number of times in this book, namely that God in his essence doesn't change. There's no 'potential' in God to be something different from what he always and for ever is. In himself, God is always fully 'actualized'. This doesn't of course mean that God cannot act outside himself. Scripture tells us that he has indeed acted in such 'external' ways. The creation of the universe is the first example of this. So, God *can* do a 'new thing' (Isa. 43:19) but – as you might expect if you've read this far – that doesn't mean that God 'becomes' something that he was not before in his essence. Even in the incarnation, when the eternal Son of God became flesh, incarnate in Christ, God did not change. Jesus' divine nature is never 'mixed' with his human nature.

Unlike the fickle will of human beings, then, God's will never changes. He knows all the consequences of everything he does. Everything that he wills to be, he brings to pass, because he lacks nothing of either knowledge or power that might compromise his ability to act exactly as he pleases. In all these ways, then, when we speak of God's acts we must recognize the infinite difference from human acting.

On the other hand, there are some ways in which human and divine acts may be compared and found to be similar. Again, we would expect such comparisons to be possible on the basis of the theological keys *God has made us like himself* and *God makes himself known to us*. Like human acts, divine acts are *free* in the sense that God acts according to his own will. God's actions really are his own,

complete *knowledge* or complete *power*, so, following the examples above, I didn't know that the door was locked and I wasn't strong enough to break it down, or I didn't realize she didn't love me and I wasn't able to change her mind, and so on.

because they reflect his character. He 'cannot deny himself' (2 Tim. 2:13). Like human acts, divine acts tell us something about the 'heart' of the agent (the person who acts). God's acts thus truly reveal what he is like. Because his acts in time are purposed from all eternity, they truly reveal the eternal God. To paraphrase Jesus, out of the abundance of God's heart, God's mouth speaks.[6] For God, to speak is to act.[7] Jesus himself, as God's last Word to us (Heb. 1:2), is rightly received by us as the abundance of God's heart.

Important though God's acts are for revealing God to us, we need to recognize that God's acts do not 'define' him. This has been a misstep (I think) of much recent theology, which has tried to limit everything that we might say about God to what God *does*.[8] In particular, for such theologians Jesus Christ becomes the irreducible definition of who God is. Theologians who argue in this way claim they wish to avoid 'speculation' about God. But they fail to grapple with the fact that Jesus himself spoke of (if I may paraphrase him for a moment) a divine heart out of which he was himself the personal overflow. Jesus was conscious that he had been sent from the bosom of the God with whom he had enjoyed intimate eternal fellowship, before and apart from the existence of the world. So, God's acts do enable us to 'name' him – he is the Creator, the Redeemer, the Father of all who believe, and so on – but they never 'encapsulate' him. God is always more than what he does.

One final aspect of human and divine action that is (or ought to be) held in common is that the *reason* for acting is always ultimately *glory*. God's works redound in his everlasting glory (Ps. 104:31). His eternal purposes are 'to the praise of his glory' (Eph. 1:14). Following this, it is not surprising that God's images (human beings) are created to act for his glory first (1 Cor. 10:31). To glorify God and enjoy him for ever is man's 'chief end'.[9] Indeed, this is ultimately for our own (created) glory, which we were made to share with God,

---

6 See Matt. 12:34; Luke 6:45.

7 As in Gen. 1:1, where God speaks creation into existence by divine fiat (Latin for 'let there be').

8 The most famous example of this approach is the work of the Swiss theologian Karl Barth (1886–1968).

9 See Q.1 of the Westminster Shorter Catechism (1647).

united to him in the closest fellowship for ever. But there is a problem with this, and it's our fifth theological key: *Our sin separates us from God.*

Biblical foundations

In this section, we'll see the biblical justification for our fifth theological key: *Our sin separates us from God.* We can't look at every kind of act that God and human beings do: that's far beyond what can be covered in a book like this. Instead, we'll focus on the *ethical* or *moral* value of our acts.[10]

We've looked already at what it means to be a human being *ontologically* (the image of God, in the wider sense) and *epistemologically* (a knower of God, according to the pattern of God's own knowledge). But what does it mean to be a human being *ethically*? Here we'll examine the biblical foundations for a view of man as being in a covenantal relationship with God, owing God full obedience under God's moral law, and as a sinner under the just judgement of God. At each stage of the argument, we'll see the biblical and theological significance of *Adam* for every other human being, including of course for ourselves.[11] In the next, final, chapter, we'll extend the picture to consider what it means for a human being to be 'saved', and given a new ethical status as a gift from God.

First, we should recognize that as God's creatures, made as his image, we owe God complete obedience. This moral obligation is a direct result of our creation. We've seen that the Bible describes Adam as a son and servant of God, and that these designations are related to the concept of God's image. It's because God has established us as his image-ectypes that we must obey him. As John Murray puts it, 'it is the metaphysical likeness to God [the fact that we are, ontologically speaking, the image of God] that grounds obligation'.[12] As is often said, in biblical ethics the indicative (what we *are*) is always the basis for the imperative (what we *must do*). Murray takes

---

10 I use 'ethical' and 'moral' interchangeably here.
11 But, in most respects, *e*xcluding the Lord Jesus, as we'll also see.
12 John Murray, *Collected Writings*, 4 vols. (Edinburgh: Banner of Truth, 1977), 2:38.

the argument a step further: 'the fulfilment of obligation consists in conformity to the image of God'.[13] Murray insists that God's *moral law* is the eternal standard for obedience. The law of God is not itself God's 'image', but is nevertheless 'God's perfection coming to expression for the regulation of man's thought, word, and action consonant with that perfection'.[14] God's law is never arbitrary. It expresses his character, and (in this sense rather like the image of God) reflects his perfection to the world.

To give an example of what I mean when I say that our very creation as God's image obligates us to obey God's law, think of the first commandment: 'I am the LORD your God, who brought you out of the land of Egypt, out of the house of slavery. You shall have no other gods before me' (Exod. 20:2–3). Human beings didn't need to 'hear' this commandment for it to be in force. It is a necessity arising from nature. Or, we might say, it is just the way the world is, because of who God is and who we are. Historically speaking, the Ten Commandments were given to Moses at the time of the exodus. But that doesn't mean that the obligation 'You shall have no other gods before me' did not apply before that time. It was never all right for Adam to worship other gods, from the instant of his creation. In this sense, the Ten Commandments form a 'natural' law, meaning that they are immediate implications of creation.[15] And, as I've said, this law reveals God. We know from the first commandment, for example, that God is jealous and he alone is worthy of worship.[16]

Man is obliged morally to God by virtue of *creation*. But there is more. Man is also obliged morally to God by virtue of the *covenant* that God established with him. I know that some evangelical Christians do not accept the idea that God made a covenant with Adam. In chapter 2 above I briefly defended this so-called covenant of creation or covenant of works. There are many good, biblical reasons to recognize that God establishes a covenantal relationship

---

13 Ibid.
14 Ibid.
15 I realize that some Christians dispute this in respect of the Sabbath commandment. I can't get into that debate here.
16 See Exod. 34:14, where this description of God is given, precisely in terms of the first commandment.

with Adam in the garden of Eden. All the elements of command, sanction and reward that characterize biblical covenants between God and man may be found in Genesis 2, so even if you don't like to call Adam's relationship with God 'covenantal', you need to account for these elements in their relationship in some way. The key point we can all agree on, perhaps, is that these elements of a covenant are not 'natural' or created necessities. They are added by God in order to establish a special new kind of relationship with Adam. Adam receives a prohibition (a negative command) in 2:17.[17] He is clearly warned of a sanction (death) in the same verse. It is harder to point to an explicit promise of reward in Genesis, but it is certainly implied by (1) the presence of the tree of life in the garden of Eden, which is said to represent everlasting life in 3:22, (2) the comparison that the apostle Paul draws in Romans 5:12–19 which requires that Adam's obedience would have resulted in 'life', and (3) the promise in Revelation 2:7 of the right to eat from the tree of life for the one who 'conquers'. We might present these elements simply like this:

God gives a command to Adam: 'You shall not . . .'
God warns of a sanction to Adam if he disobeys: 'You will surely die.'
God promises a reward to Adam if he obeys: 'You will be confirmed in life for ever.'

In the covenant, a special new sort of relationship is established between God and man. Murray calls it an 'ethico-religious bond'.[18] Making such bonds is a profoundly Godlike thing to do. If you were to ask God, 'What do you do?', if I may speak reverently, his answer might be, 'I establish covenants.' Indeed, God frequently makes his 'self-introduction' in covenantal terms. He is 'the God of Abraham, the God of Isaac, and the God of Jacob' (see e.g. Exod. 3:6). In other words, he is the God of covenant who is identified in relation to his

---

17 There's also a positive 'command' in 1:28 (to 'fill the earth and subdue it and have dominion', etc.), which I think we can take to be some part of the covenant, but its form is more like a 'grant' or 'blessing' than a command.
18 Murray, *Collected Writings*, 2:10.

covenant partners. Jesus came to establish the new covenant in his blood (Luke 22:20). Jeremiah 33:25 even indicates that creation itself is a covenantal act, one in which God enters into covenant with 'day and night and the fixed order of heaven and earth'. Obviously, this sort of covenant can hardly be 'ethico-religious', at least in the normal sense of such terms. Yet, day and night are indeed obedient to God's command (Eccl. 1:5) and the coming of the dawn is so certain that it is a pointer to the sure presence of God for his people (Hos. 6:3). This covenant still stands.

Under the terms of the covenant made with Adam, he is tested to see whether he truly fears God or not.[19] The promise of a reward for Adam gives an insight into God's ultimate purposes in covenanting with human beings. God promises Adam a glorious future to come, as a reward for his obedience. This glorious future remains a Bible theme, and we'll return to it in the final chapter of this book.

Much more could be said about the covenant with Adam, but the most important aspect for our purposes is that, according to the Bible, Adam did not act merely on his own behalf. As the 'first man', he acted as the representative for every other human being who would follow him, one only excepted. When he incurred God's punishment, Adam didn't 'take one for the team'. Rather, Adam *was* the team. The whole human race was, covenantally speaking, embodied in him. The covenant with Adam still stands, but both Adam and every other human being after him (bar one) are covenant breakers, liable to the sanction of death. That includes you and me.

We begin to see this working out in history through the book of Genesis in the way that God's punishments extend to Adam's children (3:16–19). Each of Adam's descendants *died* (ch. 5).[20] Human beings are henceforth 'brought forth in iniquity' (Ps. 51:5). All this is made more explicit in the New Testament in the teaching of the

---

19 Along the lines, perhaps, of the test in Gen. 22:12, although of course the circumstances were entirely different.

20 Enoch (v. 24) is the sole exception. His story is a glimmer of hope in the otherwise sombre account.

apostle Paul. In 1 Corinthians 15, Adam is called the 'first man' and the 'man of dust' (v. 47) and Paul says that 'we [in context, this must mean all people] have borne the image of the man of dust' (v. 49). This is something quite different from our being the 'image of God'. It is Paul's way of indicating that we all stood in Adam's line, as inheritors of his guilt and sinful nature, the ultimate consequence of which was that we must return to dust under God's wrath.

This, then, is the way that the Bible describes our natural ethical state. We were created good and upright, but now we are, by nature, in a state of sin, under a justly deserved death sentence. We've failed to give God his moral due, which we owed to him on the basis of our status as creatures. We've 'exchanged the glory of the immortal God' (Rom. 1:23) for the worship of created things. In addition, standing in Adam's line we are covenant breakers. There's an in-built bias in us towards sin, which pours forth from us in various forms of corruption, lawlessness and ever-increasing guilt before the holy God.

Crucially, *we're not designated sinners because we sin: we sin because we are constituted sinners.* When I do something wrong, my wife will sometimes ask me, 'What kind of person *are* you?' The answer (although this isn't my usual reply to her) is that I'm a sinner. That's why I sin. We are sinners through and through. Theologians call this the doctrine of **total depravity**. It doesn't mean that we're as bad as we can ever be. God's 'common grace' ensures that there are elements of goodness and truth that remain in us, and in the works, endeavours, cultures and societies that we produce. But it does mean that in every aspect of our being we're fallen. The fifth-century African bishop St Augustine (who spoke Latin) said that we are *non posse non peccare* (not able not to sin). We still do what we will, but our wills are warped. In the narrow or ethical sense, we no longer image God as we should.

Of the many terrible consequences of our being brought into the world in this state of sin and misery, the one I want to focus our attention on here relates most directly to the divine–human *relationship*. That's why the fifth theological key in this book is *Our sin separates us from God.*

The Westminster Shorter Catechism (1647) defines 'sin' as 'any want of conformity unto, or transgression of, the law of God'.[21] I've explained above that there's a sense in which God's law reflects his perfection and expresses his character. It's a particular example of the general principle that God's words – like his works or acts – reveal who he is. For a creature to hear and obey God's law is therefore to be like him, ethically speaking. Clearly, it's God's ethical will for his image-creatures that they should be like him. That's why sin, as a falling away or separation from God's law, is at the same time a falling away or separation from God himself.

We have these things illustrated for us in the account of King David's sin in the Bible. First, note the clear connection between sinning against God's *word* and sinning against *God himself*. In 2 Samuel 12:9, the prophet Nathan tells David he has 'despised the word of the LORD'. Then, in the very next verse, David hears God tell him, 'you have despised *me*' (v. 10; emphasis mine). David's own use of three different words for wrongdoing in Psalm 51 ('transgressions', 'iniquity' and 'sin') brings out various aspects of how he has treated God's law, and, by extension, God himself. Try this: imagine God's law as a 'rule' in the original sense of a 'straight stick' (Latin, *regula*). It is as if God holds out his rule for us – straight and true, or 'holy and righteous and good' (Rom. 7:12) – and calls us to 'measure up' to the rule that expresses his own righteous character: 'Be like me.' 'Transgression' (*pešaʿ*) suggests taking the stick and snapping it, breaking the rule, and in the process breaking the right relationship we once enjoyed with God. 'Iniquity' (*ʿāwôn*) means something more like bending or twisting the stick, doing what is unjust so as to bring guilt upon ourselves. 'Sin' (*ḥaṭṭāʾâ*) is often said to mean 'missing the mark' but the sense is less a near miss or a failure to make the grade than a deliberate turn in the wrong direction. We may imagine it as snatching the stick and throwing it away: *out of sight, out of mind*. Sinful people like David, you, and I are guilty of *all* of these acts in respect of God's law. We break it, we twist it and we try to ignore it. In doing

---

21 See Q.14 of the Westminster Shorter Catechism (1647).

so, we despise not just God's word, but God himself. We ethically separate ourselves from him.

The separation from God that comes as a result of our sin is not only from our 'side', as it were. Our sin means God himself also effects a 'separation' between us and him. The Bible tells us that God gives ethical assessments and judgements of created things. In creation, God declares his own creation 'good' six times (Gen. 1:4, 10, 12, 18, 21, 25) and once, finally, 'very good' (v. 31). This final judgement includes the goodness of created human beings, before their fall into sin. As son, servant, priest, regent and image of God, Adam was created holy. His created holiness reflected God's uncreated holiness.

However, God is the arbiter of evil as well as good, and human sin is judged as evil by God. It displeases him (look again at David in 2 Sam. 11:27) and makes human creatures God's enemies, so that we incur his righteous anger or wrath as rebels. Habakkuk 1:13 says of God that he is 'of purer eyes than to see evil / and cannot look at wrong'. Sin and sinners cannot coexist with the radiant purity of the Holy One. Sinners have offended God's holy justice. And as the Judge of all the earth, God cannot simply ignore sin. Indeed, his holy anger burns against sinners, and he must punish them if he is to be true to himself. If we had the temerity to ask God in respect of his judgement, 'What kind of person are you?' the answer would be that he is three holy Persons who cannot tolerate evil. As a result of our sin, then, we're constituted 'children of wrath' (Eph. 2:3), 'having no hope and without God in the world' (Eph. 2:12).[22] It is not just that our sin has cut us off from God. *God* has cut off sinners from himself.[23] We see this repeated refrain in Psalm 37, in the context of a judgement to come:

---

22 Interestingly, the Greek word translated 'without God' in Eph. 2 is *atheoi*, which gives us our English word 'atheists'. As I've argued in this book, *epistemologically* there are no real atheists: we all know God. Atheists also cannot exist *ontologically*: the atheist can strike at God only while sitting on his knees, to paraphrase Van Til. But in *ethical* terms, true atheism (the state of God-less-ness) is not just a *possibility*: it's now our *default*.

23 The language of 'cutting off' in the context of judgement is found frequently in the Old Testament. Many of these instances are passive in grammatical form, although the Lord's judgement is implied. For examples where the Lord is clearly the subject of the 'cutting off', see Deut. 12:29; 1 Sam. 2:53; 2 Kgs 9:8.

- 'evildoers shall be cut off' (v. 9)
- 'those cursed by [the LORD] shall be cut off' (v. 22)
- 'the children of the wicked shall be cut off' (v. 28)
- 'the wicked [will be] cut off' (v. 34)
- 'the future of the wicked shall be cut off' (v. 38)

Biblically, 'cutting off' may be a cultic (religious) sanction. In such circumstances it may mean no more than separation from the worshipping congregation. But often it is a more fearful punishment, sometimes used in what Old Testament scholar Walter Zimmerli called an 'execration formula'.[24] 'Execration' means literally 'to devote (out) to holiness'. Here the mention of 'holiness' is euphemistic. When sinners are execrated, they are marked for destruction. Indeed, 'destruction' or 'perishing' is frequently used in the New Testament to speak of the condition or the fate of sinners separated from God.[25] To be separated from God ethically is to be separated from the one who is the source of life and all that is good. It is, in other words, spiritual death.

Implications of the theological key

Let's just take a moment to think about the first and most obvious implication of this theological key: the **solemnity of the problem**. *Our sin separates us from God.* That's bad news. Being distinct (even infinitely distinct) from God *ontologically* is in itself no bad thing. It's not bad not to be God. It's good to be a creature of a good God, and we can rest in that. Being unable to comprehend God is no bad thing, either. *Epistemologically* speaking, it is entirely fitting to our creaturely limitations that the infinite God should be beyond our comprehension – that we cannot rise up to him but he must condescend to us. And, as we've seen, neither of these theological keys may be taken in isolation. God (for all that he is not like us)

---

24 *HALOT*, s.v. כרת (*kārat*).
25 See e.g. mention of God's 'destroying' evildoers in Matt. 10:28; Luke 17:29; 20:16; 1 Cor. 3:17; Jas 4:12; Jude 5. 'Perish' does not have God as a subject, but is the fate of those who are ethically separated from God in e.g. John 3:16; Rom. 2:12; 1 Cor. 1:18; 2 Cor. 2:15; 4:3; 2 Thess. 2:10; 2 Peter 3:9.

makes us like himself, and (for all that he is incomprehensible) makes himself known to us. We should be humbled by our ontological and epistemological limitations in the company of the limitless God, but we should never despair on their account. On the other hand, our sin is a different matter altogether. The kind of separation from God that it introduces into our relationship is ruinous for us. In addition, ethical separation from God introduces corruption into our onto-logical likeness to God (we are bad images) and our ability to know him (we are bad theologians).

Epistemologically and ontologically (in terms of knowledge and being) the fact is that we can *never* be utterly separated from God. I've pointed out more than once in this book that sinners, according to the Bible, still know God, in a sense. And God knows sinners, in a sense. Sinners also do not actually remove themselves from God's presence, or establish their being on any other grounds than receiving it as a gift from God. Even in the final judgement, when Jesus will say to sinners, 'Depart from me' (Matt. 7:23; 25:41), the place of 'eternal fire' to which sinners are consigned (Matt. 25:41) will not be outside the universe. Jesus will be present there always as Lord and Judge, even though he is not present as Saviour, Bridegroom or Friend. We can say something similar about God's presence to sinners now. God is inescapable. As Anselm of Canterbury wrote nearly a thousand years ago, 'Though any man or evil angel should be unwilling to submit to the divine will and rule, yet *he cannot flee from it*; for when he would flee from beneath the will that commands, he runs beneath the will that punishes.'[26] Or consider the psalm-ist's rhetorical question '[W]here shall I flee from your presence?' (Ps. 139:7). The answer is clear: *nowhere.*

This is why the separation from God that sin effects can be only an *ethical* separation. Whether sinners are cast outside the camp or into 'outer darkness' (Matt. 8:12), *God is still there*. Biblically, sinners don't fall 'out of' God's hands. They fall 'into' his hands, and it is a fearful thing indeed (Heb. 10:31). As sinners, we don't 'lose' the image of God, in the wider sense. We *are* the image of God. But in

---

26 Anselm, *Cur Deus Homo*, 1:15 (my translation).

the ethical sense we are *bad* images, just as we are disobedient children, wicked servants and corrupt regents. Sinners still, therefore, have a 'relationship' with God. But it is now a relationship in which he is the Judge, and we are the judged. We stand condemned. Such a relationship is, necessarily, characterized on our part by (servile) fear, attempts at deception and the relentless attempt to suppress what true knowledge of God remains. God is known to sinners, but he is known only as the Great Judge of the world, who demands an accounting from us for our sinful rebellion.

Next, we can **recognize the depth of brokenness** of the relationship between God and human beings. We must take seriously the Bible's description of the relationship between God and sinners as one of *enmity* (Rom. 5:10; Jas 4:4). There is no neutral ground in the hostility that has broken out between God and sinners. From the human side, we are best described in our natural state as 'haters of God' (Rom. 1:30). From God's side, reciprocally, we may say that God hates sinners (Ps. 5:5; 11:5). The word that's sometimes used to describe this mutual relation of enmity in the Bible is 'abhorrence'.

In Leviticus 26:15, God sets out what will happen to his people when 'your soul abhors my rules, so that you will not do all my commandments, but break my covenant'. Like David, who 'despised' God's law and in the same act despised God, God's people here are said to abhor both God's rules and (by extension) God himself. And later in the very same chapter of Leviticus (v. 30) God says to those same people who abhor him, '*my* soul will abhor *you*' (emphasis added). *Abhor*: That's a strong word indeed. The original (*gā'al*) means, in Hebrew, to loathe or feel disgust with. The cognate word in Arabic means to drop manure on top of someone – an 'earthy' expression for sure![27] This is the state of relations between God and his images who have sinned. Enmity on all sides. Mutual abhorrence.

But let us be clear. There is a world of difference between human beings 'abhorring' God, and God's 'abhorring' sinful human beings. The former is unjust, evil and utterly reprehensible. The latter is just, good and utterly necessary. As with all of God's acts, it may not be

---

27 *HALOT*, s.v. געל (*gā'al*).

interpreted without reference to God's character, and his attributes of love, justice, holiness, and so on.

So, we need to **dispense with the myth of neutrality** towards God. As a cross-cultural missionary to a people who typically know very little about the God of the Bible (the Japanese), I am often confronted with people who say they are 'neutral' about God. 'How can we abhor God', they might say, 'if we don't even know he exists?' I hope that, by now, you'll know the answer to that. Biblically, they *do* know. They have, as Paul says, 'no excuse' (Rom. 2:1). Sinners are under wrath.

Instead of loving and serving God, sinners love and serve a different master. We begin by denying our own rightful Lord, whether claiming that God does not exist, or that he is utterly unknowable, or else embracing what the Puritan Stephen Charnock called 'secret atheism': living to all intents and purposes as though God was not there.[28] In the same thoughts, words and actions in which we turn away from God, we turn to idols. This is the fruit of the terrible 'exchange' that Paul describes in Romans 1. And it is summed up in God's poetic language through his prophet Jeremiah:

> my people have committed two evils:
> they have forsaken me,
>   the fountain of living waters,
> and hewed out cisterns for themselves,
>   broken cisterns that can hold no water.
> (Jer. 2:13)

Paul links the worship of dumb idols to the spiritual service of the devil, the new master of sinners whom Paul refers to as the 'prince of the power of the air, the spirit that is now at work in the sons of disobedience' (Eph. 2:2). In executing his judgement on sinners, God 'gave them up' (Rom. 1:24, 26, 28) to their own sinful desires,

---

28 Stephen Charnock, *The Existence and Attributes of God*, <https://www.monergism.com/thethreshold/sdg/charnock/attributes_p.pdf>. Accessed 5 September 2019. Charnock says that 'there is something of a secret atheism in all, which is the fountain of the evil practices in their lives, not an utter disowning of the being of a God, but a denial or doubting of some of the rights of his nature'.

underlining the ethical separation that they had foolishly initiated. In the greatest irony, sinners utterly lost in foolishness, blindness, misery and bondage may even consider themselves wise, perceptive, happy and free.

The truth that we are separated from God by our sin ought to **drive us to our knees** to seek mercy. Even so, I presume that most readers of this book will be Christians. If that is you, then mercy is indeed yours. In Christ, we know that the truth that we are sinners is not all that may be said about us, and one day *it will be said about us no longer*. In fact, the final two theological keys in this book are distinguished from the others we've looked at, because they have a 'sell-by date'. The infinite qualitative distinction is eternal. Even in glory, we'll never comprehend God. But, glorified believers will never be separated from God again by sin, just as God will no longer draw near to unbelievers in Christ, because their (ethical) separation will be final. When the apostle Peter says that Christians will be 'partakers of the divine nature' (2 Peter 1:4), he's not suggesting that we will become divine. Rather, he's talking about this ethical 'togetherness' that Christians will enjoy for ever with God, 'having escaped from the corruption that is in the world because of sinful desire' (as the rest of the verse goes). That's a foretaste of chapter 6.

So, I don't want Christian readers of this chapter to wallow in guilt, or feel unnecessarily burdened by this theological key. But I do hope that it reminds us of what we *were*. In a similar vein, Paul speaks to the Christians in Ephesus of their past (Eph. 2:1–3, 11–12, 19), so that he can then remind them of God's merciful kindness to them in Jesus. Then, as now, that should lead us to thankful praise.

At the same time, the theological key *Our sin separates us from God* does still help Christians to **navigate our own experience** even now, as believers. Christians are those who no longer '[make] a practice of sinning' (1 John 3:4, 8). But at the same time, as the same writer reminds us, Christians still sin (1 John 1:8). There's an *ethical* dialectic here. We 'do not do the good [we] want, but the evil [we] do not want is what [we] keep on doing' (Rom. 7:19). It's one reason why the Christian life can be described as warfare or a 'struggle'

(Heb. 12:4) – internally as well as externally. When Christians sin, sometimes we feel far from God. How should we interpret that feeling, biblically?

At one level, we must resist it, just as we resist the devil and all his lies. God could not be more clear: 'There is therefore now no condemnation for those who are in Christ Jesus' (Rom. 8:1). We'll return to this theme in more detail in the next chapter, but it means that *nothing* 'will be able to separate us from the love of God in Christ Jesus our Lord' (v. 39). The sense of separation that Christians sometimes feel is not, therefore, the separation of judgement or condemnation. Rather, it is best understood as God's fatherly discipline (Heb. 11:4–11). According to these verses, in our struggle against sin, God 'reproves' and 'chastises' us. David, a true believer, expresses this poetically in Psalm 32:3–4:

> For when I kept silent, my bones wasted away
>   through my groaning all day long.
> For day and night your hand was heavy upon me;
>   my strength was dried up as by the heat of summer.

God had not cast David off for ever because of David's sin. Indeed, God promises never to leave or forsake his chosen people. But David experienced God's hand heavy upon him. That is sometimes our experience too. God disciplines his children for their good as a consequence of his fatherly love as well as his holiness.

A 'side effect' of the ethical separation from God that sin introduces into our relationship is **separation from one another**, at the 'horizontal' level of human relationships. Again, such separation is ethical: it is much more serious than voluntary 'social distancing'. We probably don't need too much convincing about this separation. It is all around us. Friendships struggle with friction and fights, marriages end in divorce or disillusionment. Politically, socially, economically – across our world, we are a race riven with divisions.

When we read the Bible, or 'do' theology in pursuit of wisdom, we need to be aware that the theological key *Our sin separates us from God* compromises this endeavour, at least partially. In the last chapter, I briefly mentioned the idea of *noetic* sin. This is the sin of the mind, or the intellect. It is the sin that is manifested in false theology and mental idolatry. We fall into mental idolatry, not merely when we worship false gods in our minds, or our thoughts are filled with impurities and evil. We are also mental idolaters whenever we try to think of God according to our own standards, rather than his. We attempt to make God in our own image, rather than accepting that reality is the other way round. Noetic sin, in its worst manifestations, is a type of wilful, mental blindness.

Even Christians, born again by the Spirit of God, are liable to noetic sin in our Bible reading. As I suggested previously, this is probably the main reason why true Christians cannot always agree on what the Bible teaches. No one person has exactly the same theology as the next person, even if two people happen to sign (sincerely) the same confession of faith or doctrinal basis. Our minds are all different, and are affected in different ways by sin. Our theologies are always imperfect, not just because they are limited epistemologically, but because they are – to a certain extent – corrupted by our sin. This should be a cause for humility for sure, and sometimes even for concern, but once again if we are Christians it should not be a cause for despair. As we'll see in the next chapter, God works to reverse the effects of noetic sin in his elect (chosen people), drawing near to our intellects and shining his light into darkness so that we can understand enough of Scripture to be saved and to live the Christian life.

Yet beyond the caveat/caution associated with noetic sin, the theological key *Our sin separates us from God* does offer us some practical help for reading Scripture and knowing Scripture's God. Namely, it helps us to **account for the way that God and human beings relate**. If we want to understand *why* human beings act in the way they so often do – foolishly, rebelliously, stubbornly, cruelly, self-centredly (whether in the Bible, or in our own lives – around us and *in* us) we have the explanation: *Our sin separates us from God*. Ethically, we are not like God, and so we do not act like him. If we want to understand, or explain, why God acts the ways that he sometimes does – in judgement, in warning, in rebuke, in 'repentance' and in destruction – our theological key is again the answer: *Our sin separates us from God.* He acts to reveal and to confirm his holiness.

In our cultural context (and perhaps in every cultural context) God's love is a notion that is much easier to defend than his holiness, or any of these other acts of God that express separation. Though it is frequently sentimentalized and misunderstood, God's love remains a 'popular' doctrine. God's justice is certainly not that.

But if ever proof were needed that our sin really does separate us from God, we find this proof at the **cross of Jesus**. On the cross, we see Jesus bearing our sin, taking upon himself the transgressions and evil of his people. God 'made him to be sin who knew no sin, so that in him we might become the righteousness of God' (2 Cor. 5:21). In his death, Jesus was separated from God. The separation was not *ontological.* God was still there, and in his divine nature, the Son of God remained one with the Father. There was no 'rupture' of the essential Trinity, as some have suggested. Nor was it an *epistemological* separation. Jesus still knew God. But, for the first time in his life, he knew God personally as his avenging Judge. He came under God's just judgement. He experienced hell's punishment and God's burning wrath. The full weight of God's justice against sin was laid on him, whom God made to be sin. This was an ethical separation, signified by the darkness that covered the land (Mark 15:33). Such a separation explains why Jesus cried out from the cross, 'My God, my God, why have you forsaken me?' (Matt. 27:46). God-forsaken and alone, Jesus suffered the full separation from God that our sin deserved.

There was no other way. That this was *necessary*[29] – that the Son of God needed to undergo such a separation – underlines the seriousness of sin and the ethical rupture it introduces into the relationship between God and human beings. *Our sin separates us from God,* and if we are Christians Jesus bore *our* sin. But the cross of Christ does not merely serve to show us how serious our sin is. There, at the cross, our sin is *truly dealt with.*

---

29 I don't mean that God's hand was somehow forced. Salvation is of God's free grace. But once God had freely determined to save his people, the cross of Christ became necessary as a consequence.

This great divine accomplishment on our behalf is at the heart of our final theological key: *God overcomes sin and makes us his own.*

Questions for reflection or discussion

1 What are the differences between acts of God and acts of human beings? Are there any similarities?
2 What is the significance of Adam for you?
3 If we are careful to consider ourselves as sinners before a holy God, how will this help us in the Christian life?

6

God overcomes sin and makes us his own

For sinners to have fellowship with God, the infinitely holy God, is an astonishing dispensation.[1]

The 'astonishing dispensation'

The subject of this final chapter is John Owen's 'astonishing dispensation'[2] – the theological key that *God overcomes sin and makes us his own*. God makes *us* his own, even though 'we' are constituted sinners. Our sin has separated us ethically from God, made us enemies of God and our fellow man, and brought us under God's just judgement. This is why it's understanding the *identities* of the Bible's 'characters' that leads us to astonishment about what God has done for us.

In this chapter we'll continue our focus on *acting*, looking first at how God has acted to save sinners for everlasting fellowship and life, and second at how saved sinners are now both commanded and enabled to act in response, in a relationship of union and communion with God.

All six theological keys in this book help us to interpret the Bible, understand the gospel narrative and know God. But of all of them, this sixth and final one can be said with most justification to *be* the gospel encapsulated. For sure, the gospel does not make sense

---

1 John Owen, *Of Communion with God*, in *The Works of John Owen*, 16 vols. (Banner of Truth: Edinburgh, 1965), 2:7.

2 Owen uses the word 'dispensation' to mean the method or scheme by which God has developed his purposes and revealed himself to man. This technical usage came into English via the Latin word to translate the Greek word *oikonomia*, God's 'plan' in Eph. 3:9.

without a right understanding of its context and significance. Recognition of 'good news' depends, to some extent, on acknowledging a corresponding 'bad news'. In March 2011, my family received a special delivery from the British Embassy in Tokyo (where we lived): a packet of pills to protect us from radiation sickness. We were glad to receive them, but only because we knew there had been an explosion at the Fukushima Daiichi Nuclear Power Plant, and there were fears (well-grounded, as it turned out) of meltdown and contamination. If we hadn't known about the dangers from Fukushima, the packet of pills would have seemed pointless. In a similar way, without the first five theological keys, we would not know either the subject or object of mercy (God or ourselves) rightly. Without this sixth and final key, on the other hand, our knowledge would do little for us other than to condemn us. *With* all of the keys in place, all that we know of God leads us to praise and glorify him for ever, for we now know him as 'God our Saviour'. God has sent us the necessary remedy for our sin-sickness.

One way of reviewing (and remembering) the content of this book is to think of each dialectic pair of chapters as 'problem' and 'solution'. In each case, the 'problem' is some sort of separation or distance between God and us. The 'solution' is a God-given means of bridging the divide and establishing relationship.[3] At the level of our being, we are infinitely different from God, but God makes us like himself, creating us as his image. As for our knowledge, we are unable to contain the infinite, but God nevertheless makes himself known to us, our 'ectypal' knowledge answering to his 'archetypal' knowledge. Both of these are acts of God's condescension, worked out through his works of creation, providence and revelation. God has given us the gifts of contingent life and the capacity for knowing him, always and at every point dependent on himself as the fountain of life and truth.

---

3 The 'problem–solution' paradigm isn't ideal. After all, it isn't exactly a 'problem' that God is God and that we are creatures. Also, none of the dialectics – certainly neither of the first two – is really a 'problem' from God's point of view. In God's mind, as far as we can tell, it's not as though there is something 'wrong' that needs fixing. So, if this scheme helps you remember the main points, please make use of it. Otherwise, please forget it!

Ethically, also, we saw in the last chapter that we are separated from God, in this case because of our sin. This separation is not merely one of *distance* but of *division*: truly bad news. But, as we'll see in this final chapter, once again God has done something about it. In the ultimate act of gracious condescension, God has stooped low to save, and he has given us the greatest love-gift of all: *himself*, in the Persons of his Son and his Spirit. Hence the final theological key *God overcomes sin and makes us his own*. This is the greatest grace of all. When we come to understand and receive *this* divine condescension, our response to God can be like that of Boaz to Ruth: 'You have made this last kindness [literally *ḥesed*, 'grace' or 'covenant love'] greater than the first' (Ruth 3:10). This really is the best news ever! With hearts full of thankfulness, we fall in love with Jesus Christ as our soul's beloved, whose 'banner' over us is love (Song of Songs 2:4).

You may remember from the last chapter that I mentioned briefly that the final two theological keys are distinct from the others because they are 'time-bound' and (in different ways) 'selective'.[4] While the first four theological keys are eternal (at least from the moment of the creation of human beings onwards) – always true at every time for every person who has ever lived – the last two are different. The fifth theological key (*Our sin separates us from God*) has always been true *in principle*. Human sin would always have resulted in spiritual death, and that was true even before any sin occurred, and even (I would suggest) apart from the divine decree to create a world. There is no possible world that God could have created in which sin would not have separated his creatures from him. But it was applicable *in practice* only once Adam and Eve really did sin: it was worked out in time. In addition, the fifth theological key was also not applicable in practice for Jesus throughout most of his earthly life. As the sinless Son of God he was in perfect communion with the Father. The same applies to Jesus now in his heavenly session, where he is now sitting down, having finished his work.[5] Finally, the fifth

---

4 That is, they don't apply to all human individuals, everywhere.
5 As we have seen, there *was* a time when the fifth theo-logic key was applied to Christ in its full force. That was in his substitutionary death as he bore the sin of others and the wrath of God as a consequence. On the cross, Jesus was separated from God *for us*.

theological key will no longer be applicable to Christians in the state of glory, when we are made *non posse peccare* (unable to sin) and saved by God to the uttermost.

The sixth theological key, *God overcomes sin and makes us his own*, is a bit different again. Like the fifth key, it's not applicable to some in the eternal state: this time to those in hell. Hell is not outside God's universe or his control, but he is never known there as Saviour or Friend. God doesn't 'draw near' to sinners in hell. In 'reconcil[ing] to himself all things' (Col. 1:20) the Lord does 'overcome' the sin of sinners in hell, but only by exercising his burning wrath against them and banishing them from his (blessing) presence for ever. Unlike the fifth key, however, the theological key *God overcomes sin and makes us his own* is not even universally applicable *now*. It is applicable only to God's elect.

In his decision to overcome sin and take a people for himself, God does not apply this mercy universally. He makes an ethical distinction between his own people and the world, choosing some to belong to him in Christ, and passing over others. Furthermore, the sixth theological key was not eternally necessary *even in principle*. God did not 'need' to draw near savingly to *any* sinners. He needed no people for himself. He was under no compulsion to choose any. He might, we must conclude, have created a world in which he did not, and he would have been no less God.[6] That he did indeed draw near, in respect of *some*, to make sinners his own is an utterly free and gracious movement of his will, so 'astonishing' (if I can put it like that) that even the angels long to look into it (1 Peter 1:12).

---

6 Some disagree with me. It depends, I think, whether we think that God is somehow necessarily gracious. If grace can be shown, strictly speaking, only to those who deserve evil, then it is problematic to suggest that God is 'essentially' (in himself) gracious, as e.g. he is essentially love. I prefer to follow Bavinck, who argues that grace is an aspect of God's essential goodness, revealed to wicked people. Bavinck, again rightly, I think, writes, 'God's goodness is much more glorious when it is shown to those who only deserve evil.' If this is the case, then *for his own glory* there is a sense in which God 'must' be gracious. But that is different from saying that God could not have chosen not to be gracious. As a matter of biblical fact, we know that his (saving) grace is not extended to every single person, even though it might seem (to us) to be more glorious for God to save more than will in fact be saved. See Herman Bavinck, *Reformed Dogmatics*, vol. 2: *God and Creation*, edited by John Bolt, translated by John Vriend (Grand Rapids: Baker Academic, 2004), 214.

The sixth theological key, *God overcomes sin and makes us his own*, is, like the fifth key, worked out **in history**. These final two keys relate to *action*, and action (at least as far as we can understand it) requires a past, a present and a future. God's work to reconcile sinners happened *in the past* in what theologian Geerhardus Vos calls the 'history of special revelation'; it happens *now* in the lives of believers and will happen *in the future* when God brings all things to their ultimate end.[7] In this sense, it's perhaps the most *dynamic* and *relational* of all the theological keys. We see it throughout Scripture, and experience its reality all over our (Christian) lives. At the same time, it's planned out **in eternity**. It was not eternally *necessary* for God to decide to draw near to sinners. But it was purposed by God from eternity and – once purposed – it could under no circumstances be stopped or thwarted.

Perhaps it's this very historicity – this *experience* – of salvation that's the reason our evangelical hearts start beating more quickly when we think of this theological key more than the others. When we hear that *God overcomes sin and makes us his own*, we sense we are in the middle of the story, and it all becomes intensely personal and real – God loves *me*, Jesus died for *my sin*, his resurrection really happened in time and space, the Spirit fills *me*, and so on. Or perhaps it's the intensity of the cry 'Save me!' that issues from a realization of the desperation of our situation as sinners separated from God, and the release of thankfulness and joy when we see that our rescue has indeed been won. These are certainly not things to be downplayed. Indeed, if anything in this chapter I want to 'up-play' them, and raise our hearts in praise. But I do hope that along the way you'll pick up some of the links with *being* and *knowing* as well. It may not be so exciting to think of yourself as the image of God or as a knower of God than it is to know yourself to be one of God's redeemed children. But being and knowing are aspects of redemption too: Christians are those who are being 'renewed in knowledge' (Col. 3:10) and

---

7 The 'history of special revelation' refers to all that God *did* in the past to make himself known as Saviour, which is recorded in Scripture. This includes e.g. all the historical events of the exodus, the death and resurrection of Jesus, and the giving of the Holy Spirit at Pentecost. See Geerhardus Vos, *Biblical Theology: Old and New Testaments* (Eerdmans: Grand Rapids, 1948; Banner of Truth Trust reprint), 14.

remade in conformity to Christ's image (2 Cor. 3:18). In each aspect of humanity – being, knowing and acting – the Son and Spirit are at work: in the history of our world, and the history of our own lives.

Biblical foundations

It's impossible to describe the theological key *God overcomes sin and makes us his own* without *any* reference to *chrono*-logic (the Bible's story of creation, fall, redemption and restoration). That's precisely because salvation happens *historically*. Christianity is not some philosophy constructed from timeless principles. As Murray says, '[T]he highest reaches of true spirituality are dependent upon events that occurred in the realm of the physical and sensuous.'[8] This makes Christianity unique. But I'm going to try, as far as possible, to focus our attention on the *theological* in this chapter. What is it *about God* that makes him the one who acts to save in the Bible's story? What is it *about man* (or what happens *to* man) that makes him fit to be God's eternal covenant partner and child? What *is* the relationship between forgiven sinners and the God who forgives sin? We begin with God.

God our Saviour

Biblically, God is the Saviour.[9] As we've seen, God was not compelled by necessity to save anyone. Salvation is all of amazing grace. But it is an entirely fitting and glorious application of God's essential love that he should set that love on certain sinners, and commit himself, from all eternity, to save them. Believers will praise him for this, and for including us in Christ through the gospel of our salvation (Eph. 1:13), for all eternity.

Salvation (or 'rescue', which is what the word means) is God's way of sorting out the 'problem' introduced into our relationship with him by sin. In the last chapter, I summed up that problem as one of

---

8   John Murray, *Collected Writings*, 4 vols. (Edinburgh: Banner of Truth, 1977), 2:17.
9   God is called 'God our Saviour' in 1 Tim. 1:1; 2:3; Titus 1:3; 2:10; 3:4; Jude 25. But the theme is explicit in Scripture from the time of the exodus onwards. See Exod. 14:30 for an early reference to God's salvation.

ethical *separation*. The separation is two-sided. From our side, we are constituted as sinners and have cut ourselves off from God. In our actions, we now tend to reinforce this separation by denying God's existence or knowledge of him, whether in theory or in our practice. And as sinners, our actions consistently exhibit our deep-seated hatred of God's holy laws, and therefore of God himself. From God's side, sin must be judged in order to maintain God's justice, and the wages of sin is death (Rom. 6:23). This death is a spiritual separation from God, which begins now and will be reinforced for eternity in the final judgement.

In salvation, God overcomes sin, and draws sinners near. The gospel (good news) is the announcement of this salvation. In the process of salvation, God himself acts in history. In Christ his Son, God *bears* sin and sin's **penalty**, and redemption is accomplished. And then God himself – by his Spirit – indwells sinners to ensure that sin's **power** is broken in their lives, and to guarantee that their salvation will be completed on the last day.[10] Finally, God undertakes to remove sinners from the **presence** of sin in a new creation, restoring to them all of the reflected glory that was initially promised to Adam and his descendants on condition of his obedience. Father, Son and Spirit work together to apply redemption to God's elect.

The whole of biblical salvation is a trinitarian work of God, in which each divine Person is involved. The Father *chooses* sinners (Eph. 1:4), the Son *purchases* sinners (Eph. 1:7), and the Spirit *seals* sinners (Eph. 1:13). Or, we might say that the Father *proposes* salvation (John 6:37), the Son *executes* and *accomplishes* salvation (in his *earthly* ministry – supremely by his death and resurrection – and his *heavenly* ministry – supremely by ascending to present his sacrifice before the Father as the Great High Priest for his people – John 6:40; Heb. 4:14), and the Spirit *applies* and *completes* salvation (John 16:14).

---

10 John Owen rightly notes that the power of sin in believers' lives is removed at the cross, just like its penalty. In our experience, it is the gift of the Spirit himself that delivers us from sin's power, but this gift is 'procured' for us by Jesus in his death. We should pick up on the inseparable bond between what the Son does for the elect, and what the Spirit does for the same elect. See Owen, *Vindiciæ Evangelicæ or, the Mystery of the Gospel Vindicated*, in *The Works of John Owen*, 16 vols. (Banner of Truth: Edinburgh, 1965), 12:520.

Man: covenant child of God

We saw earlier in this book that there's a sense in which every human being is God's 'offspring'. The Bible calls Adam the son of God, and we are all children of Adam. But the ethical separation between God and man caused by sin has disrupted the Father–child relationship. We are no longer sons of God in the full sense of those who are (ethically) like him, able to receive a heavenly inheritance in his glorious and holy presence. In the same way that we're damaged images, we're still 'sons', but ethically speaking we're 'stubborn and rebellious' sons, liable to the Father's just punishment (Deut. 21:18–21).

In salvation, we're restored to a full status as beloved sons and heirs. Salvation is God's work. By definition, it cannot be anything else. Of ourselves, we human beings are dead sinners who need to be made alive (Eph. 2:1, 5). We cannot give birth to ourselves, although we *must* be born again if we are to enter the kingdom of God (John 3:3, 5). However, that doesn't mean that we have no part to play in our salvation whatsoever. When *God overcomes sin and makes us his own*, he makes us *new creatures* (2 Cor. 5:17). He puts a new principle in us by indwelling us with the gift of his Holy Spirit (Rom. 8:9). By the Spirit, Christ himself and the Father himself also dwell in us (Rom. 8:12; John 14:23). Christians are thus indwelled by God, and made 'temples' of the Holy Spirit (1 Cor. 6:19). As such, we're not just *called* to live a new life of love and obedience – we're *empowered* to life in newness of life, by the power of God at work in us.

So, we *do* respond to God, although not exactly in kind. Newton's third law of motion states that for every action there is an equal and opposite reaction. For Isaac Newton, forces come in pairs that act in corresponding and commensurate ways. However, what applies in physics doesn't necessarily hold in metaphysics![11] When it comes to the acts of God and human beings, 'equality' *cannot* mean that

---

11 Metaphysics is the branch of philosophy that deals with the fundamental nature of reality. This book is full of metaphysical claims, because it's about God, who *is* the foundation of all reality.

God and man act in the same way or equal ways. There will always be an infinite qualitative distinction, so that *God is not like us*. Nothing that you or I do can ever equate to the acts of God in terms of goodness, power, love or any other attribute of God we might think of. We cannot 'create' a grain of dust, far less a universe. We cannot sustain the life of a single creature. We cannot save ourselves, or anyone else, from sin and its consequences.

But – and there is great gospel wonder in this – when God makes us his own, he makes us (more and more) *ethically* like him. This too is God's work, and so the glory is all and always his. But by our faith in the gospel of Jesus Christ (itself a gift of God) we're changed by God's grace from being *unable not to sin*, to being *able not to sin*. We're enabled by God to participate, ethically, in God's own holy nature. Remember, that's what Peter means in 2 Peter 1:4 when he talks about our 'participat[ion] in the divine nature, having escaped the corruption in the world caused by evil desires' (NIV). Brought near by Christ's blood and filled with Christ's Holy Spirit, we *really do* begin to be remade to act like God acts, in creaturely copies of his divine ways. Astonishingly, we become adopted sons of the Father in his Son Jesus. We are recreated as vessels 'fit' for God's mercy, and beyond that, for sharing in God's own glory (Rom. 9:23).

With the theological key *Our sin separates us from God*, we understood that the 'first man' Adam was our pioneer and pattern. To our shame, Adam both leads the way and sets the tone for us. In him we fell, and (stuck in our self-made rut) like him we continue to entrench ourselves in hostility to God. With the theological key *God overcomes sin and makes us his own*, the 'second man', Jesus Christ, takes on these roles of pioneer and pattern for us. In his blood, Jesus instituted a new covenant (Luke 22:20) in which he, as the 'second man', is now the covenant head of his people. He is now the pioneer of our salvation (Heb. 2:10, NIV), as well as the 'pioneer and perfecter of [our] faith' (Heb. 12:2, NIV). He is also now our pattern, to whose image we are being conformed (Rom. 8:29), the object of our imitation (1 Cor. 11:1). In him, believers are both *made new* and *being made new*. From one perspective, we have been given the gift of Christ's righteousness (this is called **justification**, a once-for-all declaration or 'imputation' of righteousness), so that we are now – in legal and covenantal terms – ethically right in God's sight. From another perspective, we are being conformed to Christ's righteousness (**sanctification**, a lifelong process)[12] as we 'work out [our] own salvation with fear and trembling' (Phil. 2:12).

Believers' 'pixellation' is undergoing divine restoration so that we are now being revealed as ever-more-sharply-defined images of God. Indeed, we 'are being transformed into the same image from one degree of glory to another' (2 Cor. 3:18). When I try to send a photo file by email, I sometimes discover that the pixellation is so high that the server rejects the file as too large. If I want to send such a large file, I need a better server or even a hardware upgrade. Something similar happens to believers, by the grace of God. One day, the 'weight of glory' (2 Cor. 4:17) that we receive will be so great that we need an 'upgrade' to contain us, even a new heaven and a new earth (Rev. 21:1): a 'weighty' thought indeed.[13]

The forgiver and the forgiven

God overcomes sin and makes us his own. We've seen that God does this with the goal of *covenantal relationship.* Amazingly, the Father is 'seeking' worshippers (John 4:23) from among sinners. The very idea seems like a contradiction in terms! 'Sinners' cannot worship the sinless God. But *in spite of this* God overcomes sin and makes us his own. The Greek in John 4:23 may mean that the Father 'demands' worshippers, but more likely has the sense of 'desiring' or 'devoting serious effort to obtaining' them.[14] What does it mean for God to seek and to save sinners, so that they might be his own possession in relationship? We know now that God does not 'need' or depend upon such a relationship. But we also know that God takes 'great delight' in his people, 'rejoic[ing] over [them] with singing' (Zeph. 3:17, NIV). On God's part, the establishment and maintenance of this relationship is characterized by great *condescension*, great *cost* and

---

12 Biblically, 'sanctification' can also refer to a one-off setting apart of believers, as in 1 Cor. 6:11. This is sometimes referred to as 'positional' sanctification, as opposed to 'progressive' sanctification, which continues throughout our lives.

13 The Hebrew word for 'glory' (*kābôd*) comes from a root meaning 'heavy'.

14 See BDAG for these various definitions of the Greek verb *zēteō*.

great *commitment*. All of these are expressions of his gracious love towards his elect.

Great condescension

It is already wonderful condescension on the part of the infinite God to establish a relationship with finite creatures according to being and knowing. This is even more the case when we consider God's *salvation*. In Jesus Christ, God humbled himself, taking on a human nature, and willingly offered himself to death – even death on a cross – for his chosen people (Phil. 2:8).

Jesus' earthly ministry is called his 'humiliation' by theologians. The meaning of 'humiliation' is slightly different from the way we usually use that word today: the original sense is to be 'made low'. In this sense, Jesus was 'humiliated' throughout his time on earth, from the time of his conception in Mary's womb. But on the cross, Jesus was additionally 'humiliated' in our modern sense: rejected, despised, beaten, he was left naked and almost alone to die.

Even today, there's a sense in which God the Holy Spirit is 'humiliated' when he comes to dwell in a believer's heart. When God converts a sinner, he chooses each time to place himself right alongside sin, dwelling in a place where corruption persists. Think of all the ways that you still 'grieve' the Holy Spirit who indwells you (Eph. 4:30) and you will have a sense of God's continuing ethical condescension (his making himself low to dwell with and in sinners) towards you.

Great cost

The Bible makes much of the great 'cost' to God of establishing a relationship with sinners. We were 'bought with a price' (1 Cor. 6:20). Indeed, this price is sometimes described in the Bible as a 'ransom' (Matt. 20:28; 1 Tim. 2:6).[15] All relationships carry a 'cost' of some sort. If we are not willing to give in some way of ourselves, we will be unable to relate successfully to anyone. The Bible's principle

---

15 A 'ransom' (in Greek, *lytron*) is specifically a price paid for the *release of captives*, often referring in ancient literature to 'ransom money for the manumission [setting free] of slaves' (BDAG). In Scripture, believers were once 'slaves of sin' (Rom. 6:20; see also John 8:34) but have now been set free by the Truth that is Jesus (John 8:32–36).

is that atonement between God and sinners demands the cost of the shedding of blood (Lev. 17:11). But the blood of animal sacrifices cannot really pay the required price (Heb. 10:4). No: the ultimate cost of relationship with God was the shedding of the precious blood of his holy Son (1 Peter 1:19). The price is paid by God himself, to God himself.

When we consider who Jesus is – the sinless and spotless eternal Son of God – we recognize that his blood must be of infinite value or worth. Indeed, this is the blood of God himself, with which the church was obtained (Acts 20:28).[16] God – in Jesus – willingly gave his life and shed his blood to establish this new covenant relationship with us. The limitless value of the price God paid establishes the limitless scope of the freedom he has purchased for us: an 'eternal redemption' (Heb. 9:12).

Is there a *continuing* cost to God in maintaining this relationship with the children he has redeemed and set free to serve him? In a sense, there is. Glorified in heaven, Jesus no longer suffers in his body. But when the apostle Paul met the risen Lord Jesus on the road to Damascus, Jesus addressed him from heaven, 'I am Jesus, whom you are persecuting' (Acts 9:5). There is a sense in which, when Jesus' bride (his church) suffers, Jesus the bridegroom shares in their sufferings. When the members of the body (Christian believers) hurt, the head (Christ) is also hurt. There is deep mystery in this, and we must maintain the truth that God does not suffer as we suffer, or experience change as we experience change, because *God is not like us.* At the same time, Scripture testifies to God's compassion.[17] Just

---

16 I'm aware that some manuscripts of *Acts* say that the blood was Jesus' rather than *God's* own blood. On balance, however, I think that the latter is the more likely original reading.

17 Our English word 'compassion' has the root meaning of 'suffering with'. Of course, we cannot make doctrinal statements about God based on the etymology of an English word! But the various Hebrew words in the Old Testament translated 'compassion' or 'compassionate' certainly suggest deep – even *costly* – feeling on God's part, which should not surprise us. E.g. the word in Deut. 32:36 and Ps. 135:14 carries a sense of grieving or relenting (*HALOT*). Another verb used in many Old Testament passages (including 2 Kgs 13:23; Ps. 78:38; Isa. 54:8) means 'to take pity' (*HALOT*). Jesus is of course described several times in the New Testament as having compassion in his *earthly* ministry, but in addition Jas 5:11 describes the risen Lord (*in heaven*) as 'compassionate', using a Greek word that indicates 'a very high degree of affection and compassion for someone, sympathetic, compassionate' (BDAG).

as God was at the time of the exodus – expressed in the poetic words of the prophet Isaiah – so he is today:

> In all [his people's] affliction he was afflicted,
>   and the angel of his presence saved them;
> in his love and in his pity he redeemed them;
>   he lifted them up and carried them all the days of old.
> (Isa. 63:9)

Great commitment

In the long-running British TV quiz show *Mastermind*, successive hosts have used a well-known catchphrase: 'I've started, so I'll finish.' God's establishment of relationship with sinners is like this too: what God starts, he will certainly complete. This is God's *personal* commitment to those he chooses. The apostle Paul expresses his own assurance of this truth in 1 Thessalonians 5:23–24, as he writes to the Thessalonian church:

> Now may the God of peace himself sanctify you completely, and may your whole spirit and soul and body be kept blameless at the coming of our Lord Jesus Christ. He who calls you is faithful; he will surely do it.

Notice how Paul is *certain* that God will complete his undertaking to present the Christians in Thessalonica holy on the day when Jesus returns. God is committed, we might say, to every bun in the batch. Not one of them will be burned. Not one of them will be 'half-baked'. Paul *prays* for this, and in his very next breath, as it were, *assures* the Thessalonians that God will surely answer his prayer.

How did Paul know this? Where did his assurance of God's commitment come from? Of course, Paul wrote this apostolic letter under the inspiration of the Holy Spirit. But the truth that God follows through on all his commitments was not a new one in Paul's time. God is always faithful to his promises. As we've seen earlier on in this book, that's something we also may be sure of because God's nature and his purposes are unchanging. In full harmony with that nature, and to bring about all his purposes, God has established a covenant of grace with his people. In that covenant, Jesus Christ is the mediator who brings God and people together for ever. In the covenant, each one of God's children is no longer 'in Adam' but is now 'in Christ' (Rom. 5:15–21). This does not mean that we no longer sin. As long as we live in this world, we continue to battle with indwelling sin in what Paul calls our 'flesh' (Rom. 7:16–18). But we are connected to a new and living Head: the Lord Jesus Christ, who fills us with his Holy Spirit!

For believers, the significance of this change in allegiance (or change in covenant representative, we might say) *from* Adam *to* Christ cannot be overestimated. Once 'humiliated' in his earthly life, Jesus Christ is now glorified, exalted to the place of all power and authority, which the Bible speaks of as the 'right hand of God' (Acts 2:33). In giving his life for them, Jesus loved his disciples 'to the end'[18] (John 13:1). Exalted in heaven, Jesus continues his everlasting commitment to his people.

In Psalm 110:4, Jesus is spoken of prophetically as 'a priest for ever, after the order of Melchizedek'. What does that mean? Melchizedek is a rather mysterious figure in the Bible, who appears in the story of Abraham in Genesis 14 as 'priest of God most high' (v. 18). Unlike the later priests of the Sinai covenant, who were all from the tribe of Levi, Melchizedek was 'without father or mother or genealogy, having neither beginning of days nor end of life' (Heb. 7:3). As this same New Testament writer notes, Jesus Christ is like Melchizedek in that 'he holds his priesthood permanently, because he continues for ever' (Heb. 7:24). Christians have in Jesus a covenant representative who stands before God to plead our part and to present his blood to cover our sins, and *he will never be moved*. God himself promised this permanence back in Psalm 110, guaranteeing the promise with a divine oath:

> The LORD has *sworn*
> and *will not change his mind*:

---

18 The phrase may be translated 'to the uttermost' or even 'eternally'. See the footnote to this verse in the NASB.

'You are a priest for ever,
     after the order of Melchizedek.'
(V. 4; emphases added)

What God begins, he will certainly finish. Those who have been joined to God in the covenant of his Son, and sealed with his Holy Spirit, he will *never* cast out. If Christ died for a person, that person will certainly be saved, because it is impossible that the Spirit should fail to complete the work that the Father and the Son initiated. From start to finish, God's salvation is a work of his grace, and he will always see it through.[19]

Implications of the theological key

It should be no surprise that the most significant implications of the theological key *God overcomes sin and makes us his own* are ethical. These implications concern how we, the redeemed, now live as we show forth an (ectypal) 'reaction' to the saving work of God in our lives. What should this reaction look like? What form ought it to take?

The Bible's answer may be summed up as 'worship'. That's what the Father desires: worshippers. And the biblical picture of worship

---

19 This remains true, even though it's also true that some professing believers in Christ fall away and are ultimately lost. The biblical way to reconcile these truths is to recognize that there are indeed 'false professors' of Christian faith, but that we cannot always know who they are.

This doctrine has been criticized from two directions.

1. Some argue that there's no comfort in knowing that God certainly saves his chosen people, if we cannot know for certain who those chosen people are. However, although it's true that we cannot know for certain if *someone else* is a true believer or not (although we have some hints – see Matt. 7:16, 'You will recognize them by their fruits'), the Bible suggests that we *can* have certainty concerning *ourselves*, by the witness of the Holy Spirit and our experience of sanctification. (See Rom. 8:16; 2 Cor. 13:5.)

2. Others claim that if we teach that God will certainly save everyone who believes in Jesus, *whatever they do*, we give a green light to professing Christians to live however they like. However, this is to misrepresent the teaching that God will certainly save all true believers, because sanctification and godly living are necessary parts of God's salvation, worked in all true believers by the Holy Spirit. True believers can, and do, sin – sometimes even in ruinously destructive and public ways – but our expectation from Scripture is that the *normal pattern of life* of a true believer will be, over the course of a lifetime, one of continuing repentance, faith and growth in holiness. (See 1 John 3:6; Heb. 12:14.)

is comprehensive. It involves all of life and all of ourselves. We can consider this under the two 'halves' of the theological key.

God overcomes sin

As believers in Jesus, filled with the Holy Spirit, we need to reckon with God's work in our lives as a new and defining reality. In our **self-understanding**, we must think of ourselves as entirely new ethical beings. In our day-to-day experience, this may not always feel like reality. We will continue to sin and battle with earthly weaknesses until we die. But we must heed Paul's instruction 'consider yourselves dead to sin and alive to God in Christ Jesus' (Rom. 6:11). We, 'who once were far off *have been brought near* by the blood of Christ' (Eph. 2:13; emphasis added). We remain, for now, sinners, but are sinners whose salvation is secure in Christ. Faith in God's work liberates us for worship, love and service. Just so, our new self-understanding is the basis for the biblical call to holy living (Rom. 6:12–14). The new indicative (who we *are* in Christ) grounds the new imperative (who we are *to be* in Christ).

Because God overcomes our sin, we believers are now children of God in the fullest sense, just as we are being renewed in the image of God. Indeed, this is now our primary **identity**. A Christian belongs twice over to God – once by creation and once again by redemption. God owns us first by virtue of making us, and then having once 'lost' us ethically, second, God buys us back at the cost of his own blood to make us his treasured possession for ever. 'You are not your own, for you were bought with a price' (1 Cor. 6:19–20).

The ethical call on our lives is, at its most basic, to *be like God*: to be holy as he is holy (Lev. 11:45; 1 Peter 1:16).

Does God show us infinite **condescension**? Indeed, he does – in the salvation of sinners by his humiliated Son and indwelling Spirit! Then, the response we are enabled to offer is to humble ourselves, so that he will raise us up in due time (Jas 4:10; 1 Peter 5:6). In fact, we might describe this as the 'double dynamic' of the Christian life: we *lift* God *up* and we *bring* ourselves *down*. In time, the God who lowered himself and has been exalted (Phil. 2) will exalt us together with Christ. Our lives follow the cross-and-resurrection pattern established by Jesus.

Does God pay for us the ultimate **cost**? Indeed, he does – in the shedding of the infinitely precious blood of his beloved Son for us and our salvation! Then, the response we are enabled to offer is to count – and to pay – the cost of denying self and not holding our lives as precious to ourselves, that we might find true life in Jesus and finish the course we have received from him (Matt. 16:24–25; Acts 20:24).

Does God demonstrate unfailing **commitment** towards us? Indeed, he does – promising that he will never leave or forsake us, and not allowing one word of his precious covenant commitments to fail! Then, the response we are enabled to offer is to commit ourselves to him and to his people. By the power of the Holy Spirit at work in us, our lives can come to be cross-shaped and even Godlike, in ethical terms. Counter-intuitively, this 'death' is true life. This is true joy, and a foretaste of the joy we will enjoy for ever in glory.

Again, it must be stressed that these are not 'equal and opposite' reactions on our part. Our works will never 'match' God's. But he has given us good works to do that he prepared beforehand for us (Eph. 2:10). In 'walk[ing] in them', as that verse puts it, we experience the firstfruits of the freedom of the children of God.

When the Bible calls us 'children of God' or 'sons of God' in the fullest sense, this language is not intended to exclude women. As I've mentioned, it includes the idea of inheritance. But it also reflects a Hebrew idiom. 'Sons of' something or someone are people who are characterized by their 'father's' likeness. In 2 Samuel 3:34, 'the wicked' is literally 'the sons of wickedness'. 'Worthless fellows' in Deuteronomy 13:13 is literally 'the sons of Belial'. In Mark 3:17, James and John are called the 'Sons of Thunder'. In all of these cases, sonship indicates sharing in the properties of the 'father'. A similar idiom appears in the New Testament, where unbelievers have the devil as their 'father' (John 8:44) because they do the devil's works, while believers are 'children of light' (Eph. 5:8; 1 Thess. 5:5) and 'children of God' (Phil. 2:15; 1 John 3:1) because they reflect God's character, whether shining as lights in the world (in Philippians) or practising righteousness (in 1 John).

As a believer, you are enabled to act like God. This is not to say that you lose your own identity as 'you'. Rather, it is the fulfilment (and ultimately the perfection) of who you are created to be, as God overcomes sin in your life and enables you to use all of your renewed creaturely gifts in his service and for his glory.

This renewed self-understanding, flowing from the knowledge that God overcomes our sin, gives us the truest insight into our new, true selves, and into the God whom we now know as the gracious Saviour. He is the God who takes us to belong to himself, and gives us a new citizenship in heaven where we belong.

God makes us his own

Forgiving our sin is one thing; receiving us into his bosom as royal children is another. God, in his grace and mercy, does both for each of his people. Theologians mark this distinction by explaining that God graciously gives us[20] both Christ's 'passive righteousness' (so the punishment that he endured for us is received as a payment for our sins and there is no more condemnation left for us to face) and also Christ's 'active righteousness' (so that we are treated as though the life of faithful obedience that Christ lived is legally ours). We never have to earn our justification. Christ has *won* it for us (redemption accomplished) and the Spirit has *done* it for us (redemption applied), and all while we were still sinners. When God looks on us, he sees the righteousness of his beloved Son, and he puts his seal upon us: '[Y]ou are mine' (Isa. 43:1; see also John 17:10).

Now, as justified sinners, we are 'united' to Christ. We *belong* to God, and to his people the church. He lives in us. We live in him. And we are one with one another in the fellowship of God's saints. This is our ultimate context for being, knowing and acting in the light of the gospel of God: union with Christ. Our life is now 'hidden with Christ in God' (Col. 3:3). Indeed, Christ *is* our life (v. 4). Our very being cannot be defined without reference to him who is life in

---

20 The technical word for this gift is 'imputation'.

himself. Having put on the new self, we are now being renewed in knowledge in the image of the Creator (v. 10), learning to know by setting our minds on things above (v. 1). As God's chosen ones, we now – together, as members of 'one body' (v. 15) – live the new life, of holiness, compassion, kindness, humility, meekness, patience, forgiveness, love, peace and thankfulness (vv. 12–15). Sharing in God's 'divine nature', and granted a measure of his perfect knowledge suited to earthly pilgrims, we press on to our heavenly destination, where sin and death will be destroyed for ever, with his word in our hearts: 'And whatever you do, in word or deed, do everything in the name of the Lord Jesus, giving thanks to God the Father through him' (Col. 3:17).

Questions for reflection or discussion

1 In what way is the sixth theological key in this chapter different from the others in this book?

2 What does God reveal of himself by the way that he saves his people, and the purposes for which he saves them?

3 What should be our 'reaction' to what God has done for us?

Conclusion:
theology that transforms

Searcher of hearts,
It is a good day to me when thou givest me
   a glimpse of myself;
Sin is my greatest evil,
   but thou are my greatest good.[1]

This book has been a plea for Christians to take systematic theology seriously as a way to know God and know ourselves, so that we can be helped along the way – ultimately – to participating in God's own glory and blessedness. This is therefore no trivial pursuit: the stakes are high!

To this great end, I've presented six systematic keys to Scripture so that we may grow in both *God*-knowledge and *self*-knowledge, which (please God, by the work of his Spirit) can help us to grow like him.

In fact, the keys outlined in this book are powerful tools precisely because they can guard against a systematic theology that is dry, dusty, divisive and even dangerous. Understood, digested and *lived*, these keys can foster the three 'theological virtues' of faith, hope and love.

If we truly acknowledge who God is and who we are, aware of *both* the infinite qualitative distinction between us *and* the covenantal condescension by which God has formed each of us as his images, then we will acknowledge him as Lord, worship him with our lives

---

1   Arthur Bennett (ed.), *The Valley of Vision: A Collection of Puritan Prayers and Devotions* (Edinburgh: Banner of Truth, 1975), 69.

and count him of the greatest worth. Indeed, by his grace we will **love** him, and **love** one another, as he commands us.

If we truly recognize that only God has perfect knowledge, but that he has graciously enabled us to know – and even to know *him* – 'in part', then we will learn neither to fear nor to place our ultimate trust in man, but rather to be humbled before God in all our thinking and speaking. We will be encouraged to put our **hope** in him alone to accomplish his good plans for the world.

And if we know ourselves as utterly sinful and deserving of judgement, and yet – amazingly – recipients in Jesus Christ and by the Holy Spirit of the forgiving grace of our heavenly Father, then we will go on putting our **faith** in God our Saviour alone, which faith assures our hearts that we are safe for all eternity in the almighty and everlasting arms of our covenant God.

A biblical understanding of God that is shaped by the six systematic keys outlined in this book is therefore potentially powerful medicine for us. Negatively, it can inoculate us against the twin dangers of underestimating God or overestimating ourselves. And, positively, it can equip us for every part of our Christian lives, helping to produce in us the virtues that correspond to the way in which God is recreating us in Christ. Again, this is why there is such a close relationship between the knowledge of God and the knowledge of self. It is when we start to get *both* of these right that we are on the Way of true, biblical wisdom.

This book began with a quote from John Calvin. It seems fitting to finish with one of his prayers, which we can certainly make our own:

Almighty God, in your limitless goodness you have deemed us worthy of such an honour that you descended to earth in the person of your only-begotten Son, and each day appear to us intimately in your gospel where we contemplate your living image. Therefore grant that we not abuse such a benefit through senseless curiosity but be truly transformed into your glory, and thus more and more advance in the renewal of our minds and entire life, so that at last we may be gathered into that

blessed and eternal glory which has been obtained for us through your only-begotten Son, our Lord.
Amen.[2]

---

2   John Calvin, *Ezekiel I, Chapters 1–12* (Grand Rapids: Eerdmans, 1994), 57. Cited in John Webster, *Holiness* (Grand Rapids: Eerdmans, 2003), 105.

Glossary

Note: The definitions offered in this glossary are intended to be as brief as possible. Frequently, more detailed definitions or explanations are given where the terms are introduced in the main text. Readers should consult the index to locate these places. Terms in *italics* are defined elsewhere in this glossary.

active righteousness Christ's life of faithful obedience to God's law, credited to believers by *imputation*, so that we stand as his brothers and co-heirs before God

agnosticism The belief that the existence of God (or gods) is unknown or unknowable

analogue A person or thing seen as comparable to another. (Human beings are *analogues* of God)

anthropomorphism Attributing human characteristics or behaviour to God

archetypal knowledge/theology God's own knowledge (of himself)

aseity *See* God, attributes

condescension *See* God, his condescension

covenant A relationship that God establishes with his creation. Examples include the covenant with Adam and his posterity made in the garden of Eden, and the 'covenant of grace' made with believers

deism A philosophy that says God created the world, but since then has had no direct involvement in or with it

dialectic A way of discovering what is true by considering opposites. Each of the three pairs of theological keys in this book represents a dialectic

ectypal knowledge/theology Our human knowledge (of God) that is a copy of his own *archetypal knowledge*

energies *See* God, his energies

epistemology The science of knowledge, which examines how we know things

essence *See* God, his essence

eternity *See* God, attributes

ethics In theology, the study of what is right and wrong behaviour according to God's standard

general revelation *See* revelation, general

God, attributes
  aseity Having self-existence, or life from oneself; sometimes called God's *independence*
  eternity *Infinity* with respect to time
  immensity Being beyond measurement
  immutability Being unchanging in *essence*
  impassibility Literally, 'not suffering'. More broadly, not being acted upon by outside forces (so as to change in *essence*)
  incomprehensibility Being unable to be comprehended, or fully grasped, in *essence*
  infinity Being without limit
  invisibility Being unable to be seen by human eyes (as a function of *spirituality*)

omnipotence Being all-powerful

omnipresence Being present in all times and places

omniscience Knowing all things

simplicity Not being composed of different parts

spirituality Being spirit, and therefore having no body

God, his condescension A function of God's love: his making himself low for the sake of the lowly

God, his energies The works of God, pointers (accurate but partial) to his *essence*

God, his essence God's substantial nature, who he is *in himself*; incomprehensible to creatures

hypostatic union The doctrine that in the *incarnation* the Second Person of the Trinity, or God the Son, took to himself human nature in addition to his divine *nature*

immanence God's presence in and to his creation

immensity *See* God, attributes

immutability *See* God, attributes

impassibility *See* God, attributes

imputation The legal reckoning of the righteousness of Christ to believers in *justification*

incarnation God the Son's becoming a human being in the Person of Jesus Christ

incomprehensibility *See* God, attributes

infinite qualitative distinction The teaching that God and human beings share nothing in common, in terms of *ontology*

infinity *See* **God, attributes**

invisibility *See* God, attributes

justification A legal, once-for-all declaration that believers in Jesus Christ have a righteous standing before God

metaphysics The science of the fundamental nature of reality

omnipotence *See* God, attributes

omnipresence *See* God, attributes

omniscience *See* God, attributes

ontology The science of being

panentheism The idea that there is a mutual dependence between 'God' and the world, so that the universe is somehow *in* God

pantheism The idea that everything is divine

passive righteousness The punishment that Jesus Christ endured for believers, given to us by *imputation* and received by God as a payment for our sins so that there is no more condemnation for us

polytheism The belief in (or that there are) many gods

psychosomatic union A way of describing a human being as a unity made up of soul and body

pure act The doctrine that there is no 'potential' in God to be something different from what he always and for ever is. This helps explain why God doesn't change in his *essence*

revelation God's making things known (including himself)
    general God's *revelation* (of himself) in all creation, available to all human beings, leaving them without excuse before him
    special God's *revelation* of his saving work, given objectively in his saving acts in history and in Scripture, and sealed subjectively by the illumination of the Holy Spirit in the hearts of believers

sanctification The lifelong process by which believers are conformed to the likeness of Christ in righteousness, holiness and knowledge

simplicity *See* God, attributes

sola Scriptura A Latin term meaning 'Scripture alone': the teaching that the Bible is the ultimate standard for Christian life and doctrine

soteriology The doctrine of salvation

special revelation *See* revelation, special

spirituality *See* God, attributes

total depravity The doctrine that human beings (after the fall) have an inbuilt bias towards sin and corruption, which affects us at every level of our being

transcendence God's separateness from, and exaltation above, his creation

Trinity The distinctively Christian doctrine that God is, eternally, one *essence* and three Persons – Father, Son and Holy Spirit

Index of subjects

Index of biblical references

Index of biblical references

Index of biblical references